Keepers
of the Flame
Flame

Keepers of the Flame

Contemporary Urban Superintendents

Theodore J. Kowalski

CORWIN PRESS, INC.
A Sage Publications Company
Thousand Oaks, California

For information address:

Corwin Press, Inc.
A Sage Publications Company
2455 Teller Road
Thousand Oaks, California 91320

SAGE Publications Ltd.
6 Bonhill Street
London EC2A 4PU
United Kingdom

SAGE Publications India Pvt. Ltd.
M-32 Market
Greater Kailash I
New Delhi 110 048 India

Printed in the United States of America

Library of Congress Cataloging-in-Publication Data

Kowalski, Theodore J.
    Keepers of the flame: contemporary urban superintendents / Theodore
J. Kowalski.
        p.   cm.
    Includes bibliographical references and index.
    ISBN 0-8039-6218-5 (cloth: alk. paper).—ISBN 0-8039-6219-3
(pbk.: alk. paper)
    1. School superintendents—United States. 2. Education, Urban—
United States—Administration. 3. School management and
organization—United States. I. Title.
LB2831.73.K69 1995
371.2′011′0973—dc20   95-2534

This book is printed on acid-free paper.

95 96 97 98 99 10 9 8 7 6 5 4 3 2 1

Corwin Press Production Editor: Diane S. Foster

CONTENTS

PREFACE

In the years immediately ahead, critical decisions will be made about public elementary and secondary education. Probable developments include experimentation with revolutionary ideas such as charter schools, decentralized authority, private management of public schools, and parental choice. A number of states have already enacted laws that implement or allow some of these organizational alternatives. And although these potential changes give rise to uncertainty in all public school districts, they have become especially disconcerting for school boards and administrators in urban settings.

Racked by escalating levels of poverty, crime, violence, and social disorder, many of America's great cities are described by today's media as "being in turmoil." Deteriorating conditions in these environments manifest themselves in novel problems such as crack babies and children raising children, issues and terms that exemplify the special problems urban students bring to school. In a democratic society in which there has never been a clear consensus regarding the purpose of public education, the goal of school improvement is made more elusive by conditions such as these—conditions that place many children at risk of failing even before they start kindergarten.

Those who understand the inner workings of public education realize that the survival of big-city school systems is partially dependent on the quality of leadership they receive. Arguably, the urban school superintendency has always been a highly important position. This is evidenced by the fact that many of the practices in public education today were pioneered by intelligent, forward-thinking administrators who ascended to this top executive position in our nation's largest school systems. But although urban schools were lighthouses through much of the first half of the 20th century, and although their superintendents were among the most honored and revered in the education profession, there have been only a handful of studies examining this administrative position. Even more troublesome is the fact that we know surprisingly little about contemporary conditions of practice and about the individuals who now hold these jobs.

For the most part, what we know about the urban superintendency is not positive. For instance, not only are the pools of candidates for these jobs dwindling, but those who reach this summit face the likelihood of serving for only 2 to 3 years. And we know that these circumstances exist at a time when bold, innovative leadership is imperative, at a time when the very future of urban public education is in question.

This book explores contemporary conditions surrounding the urban superintendency and looks at the lives of 17 practitioners who were in office at the start of 1993. Its purpose is to enrich understandings about modern-day practitioners—their work, their personalities, their leadership styles, and their rewards and frustrations.

I am indebted to a number of individuals for assisting with the research and the writing of this book. I thank Ulrich Reitzug, a professor of educational administration at the University of Wisconsin-Milwaukee, for helping with data collection, especially assisting with the design of the survey instrument and interview format; Arthur Steller, deputy superintendent of the Boston Public Schools and president of the Association for Supervision and Curriculum Development, for providing insights and reactions that appear in the final chapter of the book; Gracia Alkema, president of Corwin Press, for guidance, encouragement, and trust; Michael Benway, a practicing superintendent, for sharing materials and experiences he gathered in a program designed to prepare urban superintendents; the doctoral students in my seminars on the superintendency at Ball State University for making suggestions about improving the manuscript; and Mary Anne, my wife, and my four children for always being supportive. I am especially appreciative of the 17 superintendents who graciously agreed to be part of this project. They are true professionals who took time from their unbelievably busy schedules to make the research possible. This book is dedicated to them.

Theodore J. Kowalski

ABOUT THE AUTHOR

Theodore J. Kowalski is a Professor of Educational Leadership at Ball State University. His experiences in education have included being a teacher, principal, and school superintendent. He formerly served as Professor of Educational Administration at St. Louis University and was Dean of the College of Education at Ball State University for more than 10 years. In addition to teaching classes focusing on the superintendency and organizational behavior, he maintains an active agenda that includes research, writing, speaking, and working as a consultant to schools and universities. He currently serves as Executive Director of the Indiana Public School Study Council, a consortium of 25 of the largest school districts in that state. This is the 11th book he has authored.

ONE

PEOPLE IN THE JOB TODAY

What they love you for today they'll despise you for tomorrow
if you don't measure up to what they think progress should be.
—Joseph A. Fernandez

In the midst of his team's terrible performance at the start of the 1994 baseball season, Chicago Cubs' first-year manager, Tom Trebelhorn, guaranteed the media that his team would win the next home game—a loss would give the team the dubious honor of having the worst home-field start in the team's long history. He went so far as to promise that if the Cubs lost, he would meet with fans in a town-style meeting in front of a fire station adjoining Wrigley Field after the game. The Cubs lost, and an hour after the game, the manager stepped before a group of outraged fans.

Joseph Reaves (1994), a reporter for the *Chicago Tribune*, wrote about the confrontation in his column the next day. An angry crowd composed mostly of men in their 20s and 30s, some of whom had clearly been drinking, had gathered in front of the fire station next to the ball park. Several people were burning copies of the *Chicago Tribune* to display their disgust with the Tribune Company, owner of the baseball team; others were chanting nasty things about the team's general manager. It certainly was not a pleasant situation that awaited Trebelhorn when he emerged from Wrigley Field surrounded by four security guards. But although the first 10 minutes were tenuous, he was able to maintain control. The reporter attributed this accomplishment to the fact that Trebelhorn had once been a teacher, and praised him for not allowing the rowdies to undermine his authority.

Trebelhorn's action became a focal point on radio talk shows for several days following the incident. Callers seemed to be divided into three distinct groups. First, there were those who admired his integrity and ability to handle a hostile crowd. Then there were those who characterized his behavior as foolish or irrational. And finally, there were the true cynics—those who judged Trebelhorn to be a cunning individual who would go to great lengths to distract the public from his failures as a manager. But although callers disagreed about his motives, most, being true sports fans, were impressed with the fact that he apparently had "a lot of guts."

As I read and listened to various comments about this incident, I was fascinated by the fact that many fans and a good portion of the media appeared to lose interest in the explanations of the team's awful performance as their thoughts turned to their perceptions of the manager's intrepidity. In many respects, the decision to confront angry fans turned into a positive public relations experience for both the manager and the organization. But why? Professional athletes and their managers are paid huge salaries, so why should we not expect that they be answerable to us? We buy the tickets, hot dogs, and the sponsors' products. There simply would be no professional baseball without us.

School superintendents, even in our largest cities, make far less money than do baseball managers—and many would argue that they are doing something far more important. Yet these educators are continuously held accountable not only for their personal performance but also for the productivity of their organizations. They are required to stand before angry parents and probing reporters on a regular basis, and these encounters are no less difficult or anxiety-ridden for them than they are for a baseball manager. But for these public servants, there are no adjectives such as *courageous* or *brave*.

In reality, intense scrutiny and the venting of public dissatisfaction have become common events in the lives of urban school superintendents. Neither they nor the public they serve really expect anything different. Examples of this condition can be found daily. On the popular television program *60 Minutes,* the chancellor of the New York

City school system is asked to explain excessive salaries and questionable working practices among school custodians in his district; he tries to explain that union contracts limit his authority to deal with the work behavior of these employees. Or in an article that appears on the front page of the *Indianapolis Star,* the superintendent of that city's school system attempts to defend his decision to create an in-district choice program in light of growing criticisms that it has resulted in a transportation nightmare.

When the media or the public judge that all is not well with the schools, it is almost always the superintendent who is held accountable; it is the superintendent who faces reporters and answers stinging questions about practices, resource allocations, and outcomes. And no one who holds the position of chief executive in a big-city school system is spared. Unfortunately, many of these strained interactions are brought about by negative circumstances—conditions that typically place the administrators in the difficult position of choosing between complex explanations or personal blame.

Learning About the People in the Job

School superintendents, especially in large-enrollment districts, do not enjoy the luxury of controlling their accessibility to the public and media. At school board meetings, press conferences, PTA meetings, and pressure-filled moments when they are unexpectedly confronted by reporters, these educators must be prepared to deal with disfavor and reproach. They continuously find themselves in a "hot seat," and this occurs even though many enlightened critics realize that organizational successes and failures result from an intricate mix of contextual, situational, and leadership variables—not the acts of a single individual. But most urban superintendents do not accept their positions naively; nor are they bamboozled or deluded into believing that their jobs will be less difficult than they really are. Those who aspire to be a big-city superintendent almost always accept the job knowing full well that they are likely to become the scapegoats for public dissatisfaction (Murphy, 1991). So who are the individuals who seek such a precarious position? Where do they come from, and what are their motivations?

Given the inordinate amount of attention received by urban school districts since the early 1980s, it is surprising that relatively little is known either about the people who sit atop these organizations or about how they spend their time once they are there. In part, this information gap is related to the fact that relatively little research has focused on the superintendency in general (Crowson, 1987). The lack of empirical information stems from the inherent difficulties in conducting such research. Superintendents, especially in very large districts, maintain a hectic pace, and consequently are frequently reluctant or unable to devote time to completing surveys, being interviewed, or otherwise participating in formal studies.

Although as many as 50 facets of superintendent behavior have attracted the attention of researchers over time, they can be reduced to two broad categories: situational variables (those relating to context), and personal variables (those relating to the administrator). Each classification has given us fragmented information, but they have not been integrated sufficiently to provide comprehensive understandings of practice. More important here, only a few of the studies have focused directly on the work of urban superintendents (Boyan, 1988).

Forty years ago, it was rather easy to answer the question, "Who are the superintendents of our big city school systems?" These giants of educational administration constituted a rather homogeneous group—virtually all were white, Protestant males. A study of superintendents in 1958 established that these leaders were likely to (a) come from small communities and graduate from high school in towns with less than 10,000 residents (only 2% of the urban superintendents in 1958 came from communities with 500,000 or more residents), (b) hold a doctoral degree (in 1958, about two thirds of urban superintendents held a doctorate compared to only 21% for all superintendents), and (c) have moved to the urban superintendency while holding a central office position in a similar district (two thirds were already working in large districts, and none had acquired the position by moving directly from the principalship) (Knezevich, 1962).

Following World War II, profiles of students pursuing graduate study in educational administration changed almost every decade. This evolutionary process was detailed by Farquhar (1977), who created "typical student portraits" for the years 1954, 1964, and 1974. In the 1950s, the representative student was a white male in his mid to late 30s pursuing a master's degree. In the 1960s, the typical student remained a white male; however, he was now likely to be in his early 30s and pursuing either a doctorate or post-master's work to obtain a superintendent's license (e.g., an Ed.S. degree). In 1974, the norm remained a male student in his early 30s, but now about one in three was a member of a racial minority. By the 1980s, rather dramatic changes had occurred. During that decade, the modal student became a female who was a full-time teacher and part-time student (Murphy, 1992).

Because of changing demographic, economic, and social conditions, urban school boards today often seek leaders who can serve as role models and who themselves understand the social, political, and economic problems that encircle their school systems. Consequently career patterns that prevailed three and four decades ago are no longer visible; the white male with small-town values has become the exception rather than the rule.

Describing the Reference Group

The Council of Great City Schools is widely recognized as the most prominent organization representing urban school districts in this country, and given my primary objectives of learning more about the urban superintendency and the people who took these challenging jobs, I decided to select the individuals for my research from that group. In March 1993, the organization provided me a list of current members that included 43 school districts. (A complete list of members is found in Resource A. During the past decade, membership in this organization has apparently fluctuated between 43 and 47 members.) During the 1993-94 school year, approximately one in three superintendents having membership in this national group was serving in an acting capacity. Of those holding regular appointments at the time, 17 of 29 (59%) agreed to participate in my study. (Participants are listed in Resource B.)

Transitions among the 29 superintendents holding regular appointments were occurring rapidly at the time I attempted to commence my work. For example, Thomas Payzant, who was then superintendent in San Diego, was unable to participate because just 2 days after receiving my request he accepted a top-level position with the U.S. Department of Education. Several other sitting superintendents also contacted me to explain that they were unable to participate because of job-related concerns, but they uniformly expressed interest in the project.

All of the 17 superintendents who graciously agreed to become part of the Reference Group (a term that is used throughout the remainder of the book) provided a substantial amount of written information about themselves, their school districts, and their jobs. This information was collected during 1993 and 1994. Seven of the 17 also participated in subsequent telephone interviews.

Gender and Race

In general, data from national surveys consistently show that the numbers of women and minorities studying school administration have increased markedly over the past four or five decades. One might expect that this fact would have had a profound impact on job placement figures. In some respects, it has. But the gains overall have been modest, and they have been uneven across all administrative positions. In the superintendency, for instance, there is compelling evidence that women and minorities continue to be underrepresented (Kowalski & Reitzug, 1993).

In the early 1980s, a national study conducted in all types of school districts found that females constituted only 1.2% and minorities 2.1% of the nation's public school superintendencies (Cunningham & Hentges, 1982). A mid-1980s study of a similar nature found that the number of females in the superintendency had increased to 5% (ERS Staff Report, 1985). A more recent study by Jones and Montenegro (1990) found that 24% of all administrators in the United States were female; 12.5% of all administrators were members of ethnic/racial minority groups; 6% of all superintendents were female; and 3.4% of all superintendents were members of ethnic/racial minority groups. Using a stratified random sample of school districts, Glass (1992) found nearly identical percentages with regard to women and minorities in the superintendency. He established that women constituted 6.7% and minorities 3.9% of all public school superintendents in the United States.

TABLE 1.1 Gender and Race of the Superintendents: Comparing 1986 and 1991 Data From the Council of Great City Schools (CGCS) With Data From the 1993 Reference Group

Database	Year	Number Reporting	Females Number	%	Minorities Number	%
CGCS Districts	1986	37	6	16.2	19	51.3
CGCS Districts	1991	47	7	14.9	28	59.6
Reference Group	1993	17	3	17.6	11	64.7

SOURCE: CGCS data are taken from Council of Great City Schools, 1986, and Casserly, 1992.

In large school systems specifically, there continue to be strong indications that minority educators have made only small gains in obtaining administrative positions. Data reported by the U.S. Department of Education for the school year 1990-91 for "Central City Schools" (*central city* defined as a standard metropolitan statistical area with a population greater than or equal to 400,000 or with a population density greater than or equal to 6,000 per square mile) indicated that nearly 80% of all principals were white non-Hispanics, 14.1% were black non-Hispanics, and 6.3% were Hispanics (National Center for Educational Statistics, 1993). Yet these districts had substantially higher percentages of students in these minority groups.

Studying the 100 largest school districts in the United States in 1990, Ornstein (1992) received responses from 89 of their superintendents. His data showed that women were no more likely to be in these large districts than they were in school districts in general. Only 3 of the 89 (3.4%) were women.

There is other evidence, however, indicating that both women and minorities have fared somewhat better in reaching the superintendencies of the nation's very largest school systems. Research completed for this book and data reported by the Council of Great City Schools (1986) and Casserly (1992) for the years 1986 and 1991 show that both women and minorities had a greater presence in the superintendencies of urban school districts than they did in public school districts in general. These data are reported in Table 1.1.

Marital Status and Religious Affiliation

Although a myriad of statistics have been maintained about urban school districts, little information has been accumulated about the private lives of their superintendents. Periodic reports prepared by the Council of Great City Schools, for example, have not included information about the marital status and religion of these individuals—and for good reason. Such data are often deemed to be beyond the scope of "public information." Several national studies of superintendents, however, have provided statistics on these two factors. A 1982 study of school superintendents in the United States found that 92% reported being married (Cunningham & Hentges, 1982); and in a national study I conducted 2 years later that was sponsored by *The Executive Educator*, 94% of superintendents reported being married and 70% reported being Protestant (Rist, 1984).

A national sample of superintendents in the early 1990s showed that in districts of 25,000 or more pupils, 87.5% of the superintendents reported being married (4.9% were divorced/separated, 2.1% widowed, and 5.6% single). When compared to all superintendents for whom data were collected in the same study, superintendents in large-enrollment districts were slightly less likely to be married (92.3% of all superintendents), slightly more likely to be single (2.1% of all superintendents), and just as likely to be divorced or separated (4.8% of all superintendents) (Glass, 1992).

The 17 superintendents in the Reference Group voluntarily supplied information regarding marital status and religious affiliation. The mode was a Protestant who was married. Four of the 17, however, were not married (three were divorced, one was single). All but one indicated a religious affiliation, and the others identified their religious affiliation as either Protestant or Roman Catholic. From a comparison of findings from my 1984 study conducted with a national random sample of superintendents with Glass's findings in 1992 and the findings from the 1993 Reference Group of urban superintendents, some observations regarding marital status and religion can be made:

- Urban superintendents are slightly more likely to identify their religious affiliation as Protestant than superintendents in general.

TABLE 1.2 Marital Status and Religion in the Reference Group

Classification	Number	Percentage of Group
Marital Status		
Married	13	76.5
Divorced	3	17.6
Single	1	5.8
Religion		
African Methodist[a]	1	5.8
Baptist[a]	4	23.5
Catholic	3	17.6
Christian Science[a]	1	5.8
Episcopal[a]	1	5.8
Lutheran[a]	1	5.8
Presbyterian[a]	1	5.8
Protestant—general[a]	4	23.5
No religious affiliation	1	5.8

a. Counted as part of the 76% Protestant group.

- Urban superintendents are less likely to be married than superintendents in general.

Table 1.2 shows the actual responses with regard to marital status and religious affiliation. In a comparison of data from the Reference Group with results for the superintendents in large-enrollment districts in the study conducted by Glass (1992) a few years earlier, those in the Reference Group were less likely to be married and more likely to be divorced (the percent reporting being single was virtually identical in the two groups).

During interviews, several superintendents made comments about their marital status in relation to their jobs. The following three exemplify the range of responses that were given.

A lot of superintendents have lost their families, but fortunately for me, I've got a wife who understands that this job takes me away from them more than I'd like. But when I'm home, I try to spend quality, private time with them. I'm fortunate to have a spouse who understands the demands of my job. From my children's standpoint, being in a school system where their dad is superintendent and trying to make a lot of changes and dealing with unions, they experience some difficulties with teachers from time to time. I don't appreciate that.

I spend a lot of time at work. My children are grown. My wife is a teacher. This is her 20th year in teaching. She is very committed to me. We are very committed to each other, and we have a very strong marriage. And she's very supportive of me. When I took this job, both of us agreed that I would take it. We would try it and see if I felt I could make a difference and do well in the job. We would assess how it was impacting us and how we were impacting the job and make a decision of whether we wanted to stay with it. And we did that. Consequently my wife has been a tremendous strength to me. My situation may be unique. You may not hear this from others, but if anything, this job has strengthened the relationship between me and my wife. It was a very strong relationship, though, before I started the job.

Right now, housekeepers are raising my children. I'm not raising them; my wife is not. Both of us are professionals and we're into different careers. So one big issue with me is that I would like more time to spend with my family—to have more privacy and family time. But other than that, the job is fun.

Political Persuasion

Over the past 40 years, Americans have been prone to categorize themselves and others politically as liberal, moderate, conservative, or radical. A national study conducted in the early 1990s by Glass (1992) found that in districts of 25,000 or more students, the superintendents expressed the following political party preferences: Democrat, 45.1%; Republican, 30.6%; and Independent, 24.3%. With regard to political posture, 18.4% said they were liberals, 69.5% said they were moderates, and 12.1% said they were conservatives (p. 12).

Members of the Reference Group were asked to classify themselves in one of these four categories. A majority (58.8%) labeled themselves as moderates; 23.5% placed themselves in the liberal category; and only one claimed to be a conservative (two superintendents did not provide a response for this item). These outcomes are only slightly different from those obtained by Glass (1992) a few years earlier.

Superintendent data for large-enrollment districts are, however, quite different from those I obtained in my national study of all school superintendents in 1984. In that survey, 41% said they were conservatives, 52% said they were moderates, and only 7% said they were liberals (Rist, 1984). The study conducted by Glass (1992) also found that superintendents in smaller enrollment districts were two to three times more likely to identify themselves as conservatives than as liberals. But a majority of superintendents in all types of districts identified themselves as neither liberals or conservatives, but rather as moderates (61% of superintendents surveyed by Glass were in this category).

In commenting on this item in the survey, one of the two superintendents in the Reference Group who failed to categorize himself wrote, "I don't know what I am anymore." In general, studies over the past two decades have found that superintendents in larger enrollment districts are somewhat more likely to see themselves as liberals and much less likely to see themselves as conservatives.

Personality

It has long been recognized that leadership behavior is an inconstant mix of specific task requirements, role expectations, and personality (e.g., Getzels & Guba, 1957). Lipham (1988) observed that "the proportion of role and personality factors determining behavior vary with the specific act, role, and personality involved" (p. 174). Researchers studying the symbolic nature/effects of superintendent behavior have become increasingly interested in the variable of personality. In large urban school districts, where roles are apt to vary across organizations, personality is often considered a key factor in leadership selection.

In the process of collecting data for this book, superintendents in the Reference Group were asked if they possessed an extroverted or introverted personality. Only two (11.8%) said they were absolutely extroverted, but 58.8% said they were somewhat extroverted. None admitted to being introverted, and the remaining 29.4% said they were somewhat introverted. Given that most urban superintendents have role expectations continuously placing them in public arenas (e.g., the representing roles of school administration), it would seem that introverted individuals would have difficulty dealing with the exposure that is inherent in the job.

Task Orientation

Leadership-style studies have provided us with insights about the orientations of school administrators toward people and tasks. Relevant attributes of superintendents have usually been described in one of two ways: (a) along continua that range from low to high for each factor (i.e., people orientation and task orientation) or (b) in typologies that describe leaders as being either more task oriented or more people oriented (Kowalski & Reitzug, 1993). Fiedler and Chemers (1974) referred to these two leadership orientations as *relationship motivated* and *task motivated*. They contended that in each individual, one style is dominant and the other is secondary. If superintendents were plotted along a continuum with a people orientation at one end and a task orientation at the other, those who were at the extremes would most likely exhibit predictable and consistent behavior. But many practitioners are found to have more central tendencies. That is, there is far less distance between their primary and secondary orientations.

One of the survey items completed by the Reference Group related to the issue of job orientation. The superintendents were asked to classify themselves in one of four categories: *highly task oriented, somewhat task oriented, somewhat people oriented,* or *highly people oriented.* Over 80% saw themselves as being either highly task oriented (58.8%) or somewhat task oriented (23.5%); only 17.6% indicated that they were somewhat people oriented. Not a single superintendent indicated being highly people oriented.

Hanson (1991) noted that task-oriented leaders receive personal satisfaction from accomplishing goals efficiently and effectively. They are particularly concerned with giving structure and direction to events that accommodate goal achievement. It is only when tasks are perceived to be under control and personal influence is judged to be high that the task-oriented superintendent is likely to give attention to subordinate feelings.

A Snapshot of Today's Urban Superintendent

Forty or 50 years ago, urban school superintendents constituted a homogeneous group. Virtually all were white males, and most were raised in small towns. Today, African Americans and Hispanics occupy over 50% of the superintendencies in the Council of Great City Schools. And although women are still underrepresented in the superintendency, they are more represented in the largest school districts (approximately 15% to 20%) than they are in all types of school districts.

Today's urban superintendents are a diverse group. They represent a spectrum of political views, but most see themselves as being in the middle of the road. Most are oriented toward completing the tasks of their job, and more confess to being extroverted than introverted.

Before examining other facets of the lives of urban superintendents, it is helpful to step back in time to review the evolutionary nature of this position. As is the case with most social institutions, history is critical to understanding present cultures and working conditions. This is especially true in our large cities, because most have experienced massive transformations in population, wealth, and social problems. The next chapter traces the development of urban school districts and the evolution of superintendency in these institutions during the 20th century.

TWO

HOW THE JOB EVOLVED

*Did the American people get what they deserved for forcing
their educators to become bookkeepers and public relations
men instead of educators? I think they got more from their
educators than they deserved. Inadequate as most of our public schools have been as measured against an absolute standard of excellence, they could have been much worse if a great
many teachers and administrators had not been dedicated to
their country and its children.*

—Raymond L. Callahan

When we look at the myriad problems now plaguing urban schools
in America, it is hard to imagine that in the early decades of the 20th
century many deemed these institutions to be the lighthouses of public
education. Their stature reached a pinnacle during the years surrounding the Industrial Revolution—a gilded age for cities and schools
when both grew in number and size at unprecedented rates (Burroughs,
1974). Practices pioneered by leaders in the major cities were emu-
lated by school administrators in smaller school systems throughout
the United States. It was during this era that the urban superintendency emerged as the most visible, prestigious, and desirable position in all of public education.

In less than a century, public perceptions of urban education have
been transposed. Today, would-be reformers, especially those who
believe that parents and students should have real choices in educa-

tion, frequently point to problems endemic in big-city schools to buttress their arguments that public education is in need of massive transformations. Even more disconcerting are mounting observations that the rate of deterioration in many of these districts is accelerating (Kozol, 1991).

Notwithstanding substantial and continuous change in the communities surrounding them, most big-city school districts still function within organizational frames that were developed for them over 100 years ago. Thus to fully appreciate the current complexities of urban school administration, we need to understand how urban school districts and the superintendency evolved in the past century. As Callahan (1962) astutely observed, contemporary problems have a long chain of historical antecedents that are essentially embedded in two critical considerations: (a) the relationship between a public school district and its environment and (b) political realities of administering a large public institution. As early as 1900, the fate of large cities and their public school systems had become inextricably linked.

The Legacy of the Urban School System

Writers have used varying approaches to describe and explain the current conditions in urban schools. Potential foci have included demographics, economics, social conditions, and politics. But perhaps none has been more constant with respect to school administration than organizational structure. That is to say, the work of school administrators has most often been analyzed within the framework of their working conditions. Crowson (1987), for example, concluded that the behavior of school superintendents was most likely to be interpreted accurately if scholars conducted their studies in the context of actual work: that is, the specific cultures and climates in which administrators encountered conflict and made decisions.

Insights gained while studying organizational behavior have been a prime factor causing many scholars to question why massive bureaucracies, erected in the growth era of America's major cities, have endured for decades despite large-scale transitions in neighborhoods surrounding them. Their permanence, virtually unaffected by rapid demographic and social change, has been a core topic in the study of school administration for over five decades. Foremost among the questions that arise are the following: Why did these structures emerge? Why have they been so resistant to change?

The Question of Purpose

As America opened its doors to the world, several prominent educators recognized that large-scale immigration was evoking serious and inescapable questions about the purpose of public education. John Dewey (1899) was one of the first to discern that cultural diversity would inevitably challenge the notion that all children should receive a common education (a remarkable insight considering that multicultural education emerged as a cogent topic only in the past few decades). Through much of the 19th century, the paradigm of "common school" was widely accepted by civic leaders and the general public. Unlike earlier educational developments that drew distinctions between rich and poor, the common school was predicated on the objective of educating all children in a common schoolhouse under state control. Students studied a standard curriculum, and most important, they were taught a common social and political ideology (Spring, 1990). This paradigm, designed to provide a uniform education, was widely accepted because it appeared to be in keeping with ideals of equality. Less discernible was the fact that it also served to perpetuate values and beliefs of the white, Anglo-Saxon, Protestant majority.

By the early 20th century, dissatisfaction with public education became widespread, and much of it was associated with large cities. Then, not unlike today, criticisms often stemmed from the fact that taxpayers held varying expectations and embraced dissimilar goals for public schooling. Divergent views became an invariable source of conflict for educational leaders.

One voice with power during that era belonged to Ellwood Cubberley, a leader in school administration in the first quarter of the 20th century. He argued that the influx of immigrants from eastern Europe and Balkan countries posed a serious threat to the American way of life. He envisioned public schools playing a primary role in ameliorating this social concern by offering a curriculum that would Americanize immigrants. For Cubberley, changes in public schools were not designed to build a new society; rather they were necessary to protect existing societal conditions from the problems of the day (Cubberley, 1922; Spring, 1990).

The vision of education articulated by Cubberley was shared by many, especially those in the middle class. This fact is relevant because many school board members in that period belonged to this socioeconomic group. Accordingly, the reform efforts they initiated and sustained often treated education as an agency of control rather than a catalyst for social change (Burroughs, 1974)—a condition that had a profound effect on the design of urban school districts as organizations.

Building the Bureaucracy

Urban districts were the first school systems to create bureaucratic-like structures in which central office managers governed divisions of operation on the basis of assumed expertise and legitimate authority (Campbell, Cunningham, Nystrand, & Usdan, 1990). Although historians and educators continue to debate the precise reasons for the genesis and perpetuation of this organizational design, the fact that leaders in urban schools embraced bureaucracy is indisputable. Hummel and Nagle (1973) offered the following sketch:

> Educational planners at the turn of the century regarded the development of a rationally operated institution as a most important goal. Their strategy for developing and operating a school was essentially that of social engineering. The model of an educational organization and its management was a "closed system" in which rational decision-making and authoritarian control might be imposed on all the variables. (p. 36)

Many critical policy decisions during this gilded age were prompted by either the personal interests of school board members or the personal interests of those who had the political power to influence them. Thus members of a white middle class, threatened by the dissimilar cultures and religions of immigrants, directed schools toward structures that were intended to limit power and control to those who held compatible values and beliefs.

Although administrators gradually gained authority, and although school boards had fewer members than in the mid-19th century (a time when very large boards reflected the ideal of community control), board members continued to exercise a great deal of power. In this regard, Butts and Cremin (1953) noted that "more than half of all school board members in cities were likely to come from the business and professional classes and thus were to this extent unrepresentative of the great majority of people who were in the lower white collar, service, or labor groups" (p. 574). Many prominent citizens who served on urban school boards were motivated by one or more of the following considerations:

- Protecting their financial interests (i.e., their business investments and personal property)
- Instilling technical efficiency in schooling
- Changing school curricula to meet the immediate needs of industrialization (e.g., vocational education)
- Infusing economic and civic purposes into public education (i.e., protecting the interests of the middle class)

One popular explanation for the development of bureaucratic school districts is that middle-class business leaders who served on school boards believed that they could replicate industrial successes. Given the fact that scientific management was a relatively recent development circa 1910, many were willing to accept the untested premise that this industrial model had universal applicability. Powerful school boards and superintendents became the conduits for the infusion of business values into urban school systems (Callahan, 1962).

During and immediately following the Industrial Revolution, large impersonal institutions were founded on the belief that the public interest was best served by having a few educated individuals decide what was best for the masses. Many prominent community leaders believed that organizations functioned appropriately when managers made rational, technical decisions based solely on expert knowledge (i.e., decisions that were to be free of emotional involvement) (Cronin, 1973). Within this philosophical frame, centralization was not only tolerated but promoted. As a result, the institutional designs of big-city school districts became increasingly like the organizational structures of city government (McKelvey, 1969). In many respects, the school bureaucracy became a part of the even larger and more politically oriented structure of city administration.

Spring (1990) took a more systemic view of school district development: He concluded that the centralization of authority was the product of multiple forces acting in concert. Among them were the increased size of school districts, the need for the middle class and native groups to protect their values and power, the desire for standardization, and the need for the socialization of students for an industrial workplace. This perspective suggests that the bureaucracy represented not only efficiency but also a conscious attempt to deter change.

The establishment of state departments of education was another weighty factor in the evolution of urban districts. These agencies promulgated rules and regulations and enforced laws that mandated standard practices in curriculum and instruction. And because standardization was viewed as a valued objective of the bureaucracy, managers of urban schools found the general directions of state agencies to be congruent with personal biases about organizational behavior. Perhaps most important, state intervention in education helped to establish centralization as an accepted management concept.

Although there are many theories regarding the organizational design of urban school districts, it is most probable that the nature of these institutions and the practice of school administration within them were sculpted by a mixture of urban growth, industrialization, scientific management, professionalization, and the evolvement of state departments of education as control agencies (Tyack & Hansot, 1982). Further, it is apparent that the influence of these variables was inconstant across all big cities.

The Legacy

The bureaucratic nature of urban school systems persists despite decades of social and economic changes in the environments in which they exist. Virtually all big cities have had to cope with increased poverty, "white flight," escalating crime rates, and diminishing tax bases. But neither the social unrest of the 1960s nor repeated federal interventions in public education over the past 50 years have been able to replace an organizational design that continues to follow an ideology of technical efficiency.

Payne (1984) contended that many urban school districts had perpetuated what he called "pathological bureaucracies" (p. 138)—that is, organizations in which traditions, structure, and operations subvert normal and expected missions. The visible traits of pathological bureaucracies include overcentralization, unnecessary layers of hierarchy, isolation of units of the organization from each other, the exercise of informal peer norms sanctioning conformity to traditions at cross-purposes with educational goals, a pattern of rebellion from lower level supervisors alternating with excessive conformity, insulation from clients, and decision-making procedures that make it difficult to pinpoint responsibility.

Although there are continuing arguments as to whether bureaucracy was ever an effective organizational format for urban schools, there is far less disagreement regarding the contention that it is ineffective in the context of current social conditions. Writing about his own experiences as a student in the New York City schools a number of years ago, noted scholar Nathan Glazer (1992) commented:

> I have wondered why I and many fellow students in the New York City schools of the 1930s were content in a system with almost no choice, and at least as much bureaucracy (but implemented by fewer bureaucrats). There is one reason: These schools then did represent the common values of a community, the working-class community of New York. (p. 74)

In essence, he concluded that the negative by-products of school bureaucracy were less in strong communities in which values and aspirations were shared by much of the population. The problem today is that cities and their many neighborhoods are quite diverse, and that in contrast to the situation for generations past, education is not uniformly promoted within families as the primary means to a better life.

The Urban School Superintendency

The urban superintendency has long been recognized as a difficult and demanding position. In days past, however, those in office found greater proportion between risks and potential rewards. Seventy years ago, for instance, educators entered big-city superintendencies knowing that their prospects for achieving recognition and respect were reasonably high. They also knew that they might serve for extended periods of time.

To fully appreciate the circumstances surrounding present-day practice, it is helpful to trace the evolution of this leadership position. As we look back in time, critical issues in three different eras provide perspective on how the position took shape during the 20th century. During the first three decades, attention focused on whether these individuals were dupes or dictators; in the post-World War II era through the mid-1970s, attention was given to the ability to shift between critical roles; and more recently, researchers have looked at the emergence of women and minorities in this critical position.

Dupe or Dictator?

The precise influence of events surrounding the Industrial Revolution on the role of urban superintendent continues to be debated. This is exhibited by the fact that conclusions reached by educational historians who studied the performance of practitioners during this era have been less than uniform.

Differing interpretations are evidenced by divergent opinions regarding the most widely used description of urban superintendent behavior in the early 1900s—the *thesis of vulnerability*. Callahan (1962) established this construct largely from his conclusion that early urban superintendents were the political pawns of the rich and powerful. Looking closely at the tenure of several big-city superintendents, he judged that those holding office from approximately 1910 to 1930 were intimidated by strong-willed and persuasive school board members who believed that principles of scientific management were ideal for all organizations. Widely accepted, Callahan's thesis has been cited in literally hundreds of manuscripts describing the formative years of urban school districts. Recently, however, several authors have questioned the accuracy of his conclusion.

One challenge is predicated on time parameters. Berman (1983) concluded that Callahan's supposition was flawed because urban school districts had already institutionalized bureaucracy by 1910 as a result of mid-19th-century developments (most notably demands for school reform). Accordingly, she concluded that rather than describing products of the Industrial Revolution, Callahan was actually analyzing the repercussions of decisions made some 30 to 40 years earlier.

Button (1991) disputed both Callahan's thesis and Berman's exceptions to it. He greeted with skepticism Berman's conclusion that bureaucracy became institutionalized as early as the mid-1800s, and he did so essentially on the grounds of impact. That is, Button judged that even though aspects of bureaucracy might have been put in place prior to 1910, the overall acceptance of this organizational design, and hence its impact on educational operations, had been slight. His concerns with Callahan's analysis centered on the question of whether the theory of vulnerability was sufficiently comprehensive to account for superintendent behavior. He noted that many administrators during this era sought higher status, and that their primary strategy for achieving status was to model behaviors of managers who had acquired respect and power in industrial circles. More specifically, Button deduced that the image of superintendent as business executive may have had more to do with emulation than vulnerability. This perspective portrays superintendents of that era more as cunning politicians than as helpless dupes.

Yet another, but similar, challenge to the theory of vulnerability is found in the work of Thomas and Moran (1992). Examining the tenure of Ernest Hartwell, who served as superintendent in St. Paul, Minnesota, and Buffalo, New York, during the early 1920s, they reasoned that this superintendent used scientific management not because he felt compelled to do so, but rather as a means to protect the power he already possessed. They described several behaviors that led them to this conclusion:

> During his superintendencies, Hartwell fired militant teachers and principals when they challenged his authority to implement widely prescribed school reforms that proved to be beneficial to his reputation. Adopting a business model of management and applying new state laws to his advantage, this superintendent enlarged the school bureaucracy to increase his supervision over teachers and to isolate himself further from political adversaries. (p. 48)

Both this profile and Button's thesis of emulation suggest that it was personal values, beliefs, and needs that led some superintendents to establish bureaucratic-like structures, and that rather than being vulnerable, they were actually skillful individuals capable of manipulating people and groups to protect their personal interests.

Another group of writers (e.g., Burroughs, 1974; Tyack, 1972) questioned the thesis of vulnerability on the grounds that a number of urban superintendents accepted bureaucracy largely because it was politically advantageous for them to do so. Rather than seeing these school leaders as pawns, these writers judged many urban superintendents during the Industrial Revolution era to have been intelligent, sensitive, and discriminating educators. Confronted with big-city politics and powerful school boards, they realized that their levels of responsibility and authority were ill balanced. Tyack (1972) offered the following description of those times: "During the latter half of the nineteenth century, superintendents were trapped between their vision of 'the one best system' of school bureaucracy and the political realities of their positions. Even those who had served long and devotedly were often unceremoniously fired. For many the job was a revolving door" (p. 241). Thus many big-city superintendents overtly embraced the dream of being able to construct rational, efficient institutions not because they were cowards or ignorant, but rather because their political skills indicated that there was no reasonable alternative.

These varying images of early urban superintendents are partially explained by the fact that those who examine history are never devoid of personal bias and philosophy (Eaton, 1990). A clear example of this effect is found in the conflicting perceptions of historical reality contained in Callahan's *Education and the Cult of Efficiency* (1962) and Lawrence Cremin's *The Transformation of the School* (1961). The two books examined the same period of educational history, they were published within a year of each other, and each was praised by prominent scholars as a monumental contribution to the professional literature. Yet the two books put forward distinctively different viewpoints of school district development (Schaefer, 1990).

To categorize all urban superintendents during the developmental years as dupes would be both unfair and inaccurate. Nor is it appropriate to label all of them as ruthless dictators or professionally committed scholars. Historians find that they cannot easily separate fears of big-city politics and corruption from a quest for status and power or the influence of school board members from prevailing social conditions. Each of these factors had some impact on superintendent behavior, and surely the mix was unique from city to city. Exact analysis is made even more complex by the realization that every educator who ascended to this high position brought individually developed interests, talents, needs, wants, and motivations to the job.

Griffiths (1966) contended that the image of superintendent as business executive reached its zenith toward the end of the 1920s. After 1930, there was a gradual shift toward emphasizing the principles of democratic administration, a transition that paralleled the human relations movement in private industry. But discussions among intellectuals and practitioners failed to eradicate long-standing perceptions held by school superintendents: "Although the introduction of democracy as an ideology had some effect on superintendents, it is not possible to say it did mediate the strong thrust towards the businessman stereotype" (Griffiths, 1966, p. 32). So notwithstanding changes in the ecosystems surrounding big-city public schools and calls from within the profession for reconceptualizations of organizational leadership that would be more congruent with life in a democratic society, many practitioners continued to adhere to a model of management that evolved in the formative days of school administration.

Differing Expectations

Studies of the evolution of urban school districts make it apparent that many educational leaders had difficulty defining their own roles. Cuban (1976) noted that three distinctively separate conceptions of "ideal leader" could be found in the writings and speeches of early superintendents. These conceptions, which recurred from 1870 to approximately 1950, were

- *Teacher-Scholar* (educational specialist)
- *Administrative Chief* (manager, specialist in scientific management, and authoritarian)
- *Negotiator-Statesman* (the person who generates support from diverse groups and resolves conflict)

Employing these classifications as an analytical framework, Cuban conducted an ethnographic study of three prominent urban superintendents who were in office during the 1960s. They were Ben Willis in Chicago, Carl Hansen in Washington, D.C., and Harold Spears in San Francisco. Cuban concluded that parts of the three conceptions could be found in each of these leaders, but the degree to which they were present was both dynamic and uneven. He wrote, "Not completely helpless, urban superintendents adopted diverse philosophies to help them cope with an unpredictable environment; some conceptions proved more durable than others at certain times, but none disappeared, for they were inherent to the nature of the job" (p. 139). The three superintendents were in a constant crossfire of expectations, requests, and demands, and in the final analysis, changes in the cities in which they worked eroded the support they had initially enjoyed from their school boards.

Cuban's (1976) analysis, especially his observation that these individuals were capable of wearing different hats, was not unlike observations made by other scholars who had studied superintendents. Both Burroughs (1974) and Tyack (1972) also noted a tendency for top executives in large school districts to be rather pragmatic. These administrators were able to make adaptations in their behavior and time commitments when organizational or community conditions suggested that such changes were either advantageous or necessary.

The Emergence of Women and Minorities

At the time that urban school districts were taking shape, the public generally treated teaching as an occupation for women and administration as an occupation for men. Ortiz and Marshall (1988) wrote:

The history of the formative years of education uncovers the processes and the meaning of the development of a social system in which men secured and continue to retain control of the power structures, women's roles are undermined, and administration is separated from teaching. The story also reveals how municipal reform and admiration for the corporate executive model helped to establish administration as the more valuable, powerful, and responsible of the two mutually dependent professions. (p. 125)

To fully appreciate the ethos of that era, we need to recognize that males constituted a majority in two critical groups: (a) school board members, and (b) professors of educational administration. These conditions contributed to a situation in which male school administrators were more acceptable to the powerful figures who controlled community life (Tyack & Hansot, 1982).

Education professors played a prominent role in trying to gain professional recognition for their discipline. Many who specialized in administration saw scientific management as an opportunity to achieve that goal. The fact that the quests for professionalism and efficiency occurred at approximately the same time in history is certainly relevant. Especially in urban districts, the two objectives became squarely joined, and products of their union constituted a potent force in determining organizational structure and administrator behavior. The two intertwined to an extent that made it impossible to precisely describe their separate influence, but their product was obvious. Administration and teaching were cast as distinctive occupations, the former requiring specialized knowledge in management and personal characteristics that met the image of a manager, such as a stern, objective disposition. And the role of school superintendent was especially molded to fit these specifications.

Survey data gathered over the past 100 years provide a rather consistent picture of the individuals who have occupied the top administrative positions in the largest districts. As noted in the previous chapter, they were nearly all white males, married, highly experienced, and Protestants who were active in their churches. In their enlightening book *Managers of Virtue*, Tyack and Hansot (1982) offered the following explanation: "The very ambiguity and diffuseness of the goals of schooling, and the consequent difficulty of measuring 'success' or 'failure,' probably reinforced the significance of maleness, mature age, 'proper' ethnicity, acceptable church membership, and appearance (not surprisingly, superintendents were taller than average, giving people someone to look up to)" (p. 170). And nowhere were complexity and chaos greater concerns than in the urban schools. A preoccupation with goals such as moral respectability and social stability diverted public attention from the fact that the purposes of public education remained largely unsettled. In the midst of this inconstancy, it was politically comforting to have school leaders who exuded confidence—administrators who looked and acted like able managers.

Although women have dominated the workforce in education for at least the last 75 years, their ability to ascend to the highest positions of authority has been limited. During the 1974-75 school year, a mere 1% of the nation's superintendents were female (Paddock, 1981). Comparing employment in urban and rural districts, Jacobson (1989) reported that women were twice as likely to be employed as administrators in urban environments as in other types of communities. Since the passage of civil rights laws (legislation that ironically reduced the number of African American administrators because of the eventual closing of segregated schools), similar conditions have existed for minority superintendents.

Demands made of minorities and women in the urban superintendency are particularly noteworthy. Although there is no evidence suggesting that they were excused from any of the common role expectations and responsibilities of the position, there are indications that their ideal roles have been unique. Unlike their white, male counterparts, they often have had to assume additional obligations that are products of more subtle forms of stereotypical race and gender-driven perceptions. For instance, school board members may expect that a female superintendent will be less interested in personal power, and thus more willing to abandon aspects of bureaucracy—for example, less likely to rely on legitimate authority and more willing to implement aspects of decentralization (Kowalski & Reitzug, 1993).

Likewise, minority educators have commonly faced expectations that are largely race related. For instance, African American superintendents may be expected to bring a cultural awareness and valence to the superintendency that prompts them to challenge current and past practices. Reflecting on African American superintendents in the late 1980s, Scott (1990) suggested that these administrators might be the last hope for thousands of African American students to receive equal educational opportunity: "It is hoped that the integration of Black consciousness and professionalism by Black superintendents will save Black communities from the repugnant circumstances of replacing ineffective, predominately White bureaucracies with Black-controlled bureaucracies of the same disposition" (p. 172). Expectations such as these, although understandable, nevertheless intensify job pressures placed on minority and female urban superintendents.

Opportunities for women and minorities to enter the urban superintendency have increased ever since the late 1960s. During this period, however, the position became more difficult, risk laden, and undesirable; and some observers believe that these circumstances have, in part, enhanced the prospects of female and minority applicants. It is certainly significant that their opportunities to reach this prominent position have come at a time when the revolving door to the superintendent's office is spinning at an ever more rapid pace.

Concluding Thoughts

Urban districts and the urban school superintendency evolved in an era that stands in sharp contrast to contemporary conditions. They were fashioned when cities were expanding rapidly, America was moving toward an industrial economy, educational administration was struggling to become a profession, and demands for reform cast schools as agencies of control rather than as instruments for social change. During this era, bureaucratic ideals were embraced, and school administrators sought recognition as professionals by portraying themselves as stable, capable, and respectable managers.

Despite immense demographic, political, and economic changes in America's largest cities, many observers believe that urban school districts have remained organized much as they were in the early 1920s. This has resulted in an ever-expanding gap between real educational needs that exist in urban America and failed traditional approaches to schooling that are predicated largely on the quest for the efficient delivery of a uniform curriculum. In less than a century, the image of urban education has been transformed from one of innovation to one of inertia—and the implications for those who assume the top administrative position of these school districts have been profound.

Even though it can be argued that urban superintendents have always assumed a political role, the nature and intensity of this aspect of the job have not remained constant over time. Legislative and judicial interventions have pushed public education into the arena of hardnosed politics. For example, urban school boards have become conscious of creating racial, ethnic, and social class balance, and although the goal is laudable, the efforts have often generated factionalism (Ortiz, 1991).

As urban conditions worsened, especially since 1960, the door to the superintendency became more open to two groups of individuals who historically had been underrepresented in the position—women and minorities. Unfortunately, however, their opportunities have expanded over the same period that the big cities have deteriorated.

THREE

A Look at Job Conditions

Superintendents who do not use their office to lead will create a school system incapable of leadership in the community.
—Philip C. Schlechty

In recent years, the public's dissatisfaction with urban education has often been directed at administrators, a proclivity that affects both those in top-level positions and those who aspire to acquire them. Although it is readily apparent that the average tenure of urban superintendents is quite short, it is far less understood that this situation is made more disconcerting by dwindling pools of applicants (Jackson & Cibulka, 1992). In the context of what seem to be insurmountable economic and social problems, there simply are fewer and fewer highly qualified school administrators pursuing the job that was once considered the most powerful in public education.

This chapter examines two controversial topics. The first is urban superintendents' length of service and potential explanations as to why the average tenure of these executives is so brief. The second is compensation.

Length of Service

Rapid turnover in the urban superintendency is not exactly a recent development. During the period of 1970 to 1973, for example, 23 of the

25 largest school systems in America appointed new superintendents (Cuban, 1976). Data collected for the 1985-86 school year from 37 school districts then making up the Council of Great City Schools indicated that the average tenure for member superintendents was approximately 4 years—and that five of the superintendents in the council had been in office for more than 10 years (Council of Great City Schools, 1986). In a 1990 study, Jackson and Cibulka (1992) found that the average tenures of urban superintendents ranged from 3 to 5 years. The Council of Great City Schools (1992) reported that as of 1992, 68% of the 47 superintendents had been appointed since 1989, and seven who were appointed prior to 1989 had already announced their retirements effective the end of the 1991-92 school year.

An early 1990s study conducted by Glass (1992) for the American Association of School Administrators found that superintendents in the nation's 20 largest districts stay an average of 2.5 years compared with an average of 6.2 years for all superintendents. Renchler (1992) also reported an average tenure of 2.5 years for urban superintendents compared to a national average of 5.6 years for all superintendents. In his survey of 89 superintendents in school systems with enrollments over 33,500 students in 1990, Ornstein (1992) found that one in four had 1 year or less in his or her current position. Slightly fewer than 7% had managed to survive 11 or more years. In surveying superintendents in school districts with over 25,000 students in 1990, Glass (1992) reported that only about one in three had been in his or her current position for more than 5 years. By the end of 1992, for example, 77% of the superintendents in districts making up the Council of Great City Schools had been hired since 1990 (Casserly, 1992). In 1993, 40 of the nation's largest 45 school districts had superintendents who had been appointed during or after 1990 (Jordan, 1993).

Data from the Reference Group showed that approximately three out of four superintendents had been in their current positions less than 3 years. Of the remaining four who had longer tenures, one had been in the position 4 years, one for 5 years, one for 10 years, and one for 13 years. The average tenure for the group was approximately 3.5 years, but when the two highest tenures were excluded, that average dropped to only 2.3 years. Two of the superintendents were completing their first year when the study was conducted.

The revolving door to the big-city superintendent's office not only has negative implications for those who occupy the office but also deters long-range planning and change within the organization. A discussion among 20 urban superintendents in 1990 revealed a prevailing concern that districts were essentially unable to move forward; an average life span of 2.5 years simply did not permit superintendents to effect meaningful change (Renchler, 1992).

Nowhere is the revolving door to the superintendent's office more evident than in the nation's largest school district. In early April 1994, Ramon Cortines, following a disagreement with the newly elected mayor, Rudolph Giuliani, submitted his resignation as chancellor of the New York City schools after having served less than 1 year. The school system has had 12 superintendents in less than 25 years; even more revealing, the 7 most recent chancellors served an average of 14 months (Winerip, 1994). Weeks later, however, the mayor and Cortines resolved their differences over fiscal controls, and the superintendent withdrew his resignation.

Reasons for Rapid Turnover

Analysts have cited a number of reasons for the increasingly short tenure of urban superintendents. Jackson and Cibulka (1992) attributed the accelerating turnover rate to a shift from demands for racial equity to concerns for overall educational quality. This, they said, had created an "inability to manage growing demands for excellence, resulting in leadership turnover and problems of superintendent recruitment" (p. 84). They further observed that the "demands for greater accountability and quality are not new" but argued that "a new activism by business leaders" (p. 84) had resulted in increased pressure for quality schooling and superintendent accountability.

Other analysts have offered different interpretations. Rist (1990) attributed rapid turnover to "heightened racial and ethnic-group politics and increasingly rocky board-superintendent relations" (p. 12). She cited the no-win situations in which both white and African American superintendents find themselves in trying to address the needs of largely minority-attended urban public schools. White superintendents, she noted, "face an 'implicit challenge' from staff members and community groups alike" (p. 13), due to the racial and cultural differences between them and their constituents. African American superintendents, on the other hand, "often believe their authority is questioned by the white power structure in the community" (p. 13). In addition, Rist noted that many believe minority candidates do not attain urban superintendencies until the district has "deep-seated, nearly intractable problems" (p. 13). A decade earlier, in his development of case studies of seven African American superintendents during the 1970s, Scott (1980) had already concluded that poverty, low academic achievement, social problems, and fiscal inadequacies were discouraging many white candidates from pursuing urban superintendencies.

David Bennett (1991), former superintendent of the Minneapolis Public Schools, offered a different set of reasons for rapid urban superintendent turnover. They included the following:

- The politicization of urban school boards (i.e., their interest in pleasing their immediate constituencies rather than in doing what is good for the whole district)
- The "impossible job" syndrome (i.e., when the new superintendent who is generally hailed as a "savior" is unable to find instant solutions, the board quickly becomes disappointed and dissatisfied)
- A decline in missionary zeal (Bennett, 1991, noted, "At one time, urban superintendent candidates had an almost missionary notion of service to urban schoolchildren," p. 24)
- A lack of training (i.e., few legitimate preparation programs for the urban superintendency exist)
- Better opportunities elsewhere (i.e., in better paying, less troublesome metropolitan districts)
- Racial tensions (i.e., challenges to the authority of white superintendents from their largely minority constituencies)
- "Role confusion" (i.e., conflict generated by state education authorities setting policy—formerly the purview of school boards—and school boards administering—formerly the purview of superintendents)

Perhaps the two most common reasons given for frequent changes in the superintendency pertain to irreconcilable conflict and upward mobility. Ornstein (1992) concluded about large district school superintendents that "they either clash with school boards, especially as original supporters are replaced with new members, or the grass seems greener elsewhere and they get the urge to move on" (p. 157). Historically, many school administrators accepted the reality of changing employers in order to seek advancement; hence relocation was for them an inevitable aspect of career development. And with the constant likelihood of serious conflict, insecurity often prompted these individuals to keep a constant eye on the job market.

The turnover of urban superintendents has often been analyzed in the context of politics and stress. Political conflict, in particular, has been a popular topic among school administration scholars, and "dissatisfaction theory" has emerged as a paradigm that some have used to draw connections between the defeat of incumbent school board members and the subsequent departure of the superintendent (e.g., Rada, 1984). More broadly, the theory focuses on a chain of four events— community dissatisfaction, incumbent school board members' being defeated, superintendent turnover, and an outsider's becoming the new superintendent. Hosman (1990) described the foundation of the theory:

> The theory was based on the hypothesis that the school board and the superintendent, having similar values, become a closed decision-making system that becomes, with increasing stability and internal consistency, unaware of or unresponsive to the demands of a changing community; if the unsatisfied demands become great enough, they precipitate increased political activity, and incumbent board members are defeated. (p. 351)

But after a number of studies, critics remain unconvinced that such theories adequately explain how conflict evolves as a critical factor in superintendent turnover.

Larry Cuban, who has written extensively on the topic of urban superintendents, offered a more direct explanation that also emphasized organizational-environmental tensions. He suggested that high turnover may be linked to cycles of intense stress. When money is scarce, expectations for schools high, and communities are changing, urban school chiefs are likely to experience higher levels of stress, and it is during these periods that turnover is most rapid (Goldstein, 1992). In a 1993 interview with a *Washington Post* reporter, Michael Casserly, executive head of the Council of Great City Schools, echoed these sentiments when he noted that the high turnover rate among urban superintendents was, in part, due to hysteria spawned by demands for reform. He sensed that the public desperately wanted immediate results, but warned that immediate results don't happen in education (Jordan, 1993).

Insecurity and Loyalty

Even though high insecurity is a reality in the urban superintendency, this fact rarely diminishes expectations of loyalty—loyalty to the school board, the mayor, and the school district. It is in many ways a very awkward position in which to find oneself. The superintendents are in a profession in which mobility has been a common path to higher paying jobs, and they face conflicts and must take risks that undermine their ability to survive for more than 3 or 4 years. Yet when they explore new career opportunities, they usually create tension in their relationships with school boards and other community leaders. Thus they are forced to walk a career tightrope: They know that it is to their advantage to keep an eye open for advancement opportunities, but they must do it very discreetly.

Consider a late-1993 incident involving Shirl Gilbert, former superintendent of the Indianapolis Public Schools. On December 3, the *Indianapolis Star*, the city's largest newspaper, claimed in a front-page story that Gilbert had applied for a superintendency in Broward County, Florida. The next day, the paper carried a second article on the same topic, based largely on an interview with Gilbert. The reporter (Penner, 1993) noted that Gilbert had faxed letters to selected community leaders reassuring them that he remained committed to his job in Indianapolis and stating that the news story of the previous day was misleading.

In the interview, Gilbert tried to counter suggestions that he was an applicant for the Florida superintendency. He explained that Floretta McKenzie, a long-time friend and consultant to the school district in Florida, had convinced him to have his name submitted to the Broward

County School Board. After a 45-minute telephone conversation with her, he had consented to have his resume submitted but had emphasized that he was not interested in the job. The reporter asked Dr. Gilbert why he hadn't just said "no." Gilbert said he had, and emphasized that he had done nothing overtly to pursue this job. The article pointed out, however, that he also had done nothing overtly to not pursue the job, such as formally withdrawing his name. When the reporter asked him what he would do if the Broward County School Board requested a formal application or asked him to go to Florida for an interview, Gilbert responded that he would not answer questions based on conjecture.

The same article contained comments from Gilbert's board president, Stephen J. Hyatt, expressing a common perception that board members have of superintendents. It was irrelevant, said Hyatt, whether Gilbert applied or was nominated; superintendents were always looking for the next job. Explaining that Gilbert had come to Indianapolis from a smaller district, the board president added that moving to an even larger district was a natural progression in the superintendent's career.

On December 8, Gilbert and the Broward County position again made the front page of the *Indianapolis Star*. This time, the story relayed the news that although Gilbert had been named one of the eight finalists for the Florida position, he had formally withdrawn his name— he now had done something overtly to assure the public that he no longer was a candidate (Rochester, 1993). Just 4 months later, the May 18, 1994, headline of the *Indianapolis Star* notified readers that Gilbert had resigned as head of the Indianapolis Public Schools. But on May 21, in a special session, his school board voted four to three to dismiss him before he had submitted his formal letter of resignation (Penner & Hooper, 1994).

Reference Group Comments
on Turnover and Survival

Both ambition and conflict were quite evident in comments provided by members of the Reference Group when discussing turnover among their peers. One said that the superintendents themselves were to blame for the declining average tenure. He was convinced that personal interests often prevented superintendents from making a strong commitment to their current employers.

> I think when you look at the turnover in the urban superintendency, there are many variables to consider. I was reading some research a couple of weeks ago that suggested that many superintendents were leaving on their own. Not because of their school boards—but because they are greedy. They want to move just like the Methodist ministers—to bigger school districts. As urban superintendents, we ought to commit 5 to 10 years. I'm not looking for another job. I told my board, I plan to retire here. Urban superintendents should make a commitment up front; then their communities can't accuse them of using their job as a stepping stone.

The extent of peer criticism in comments about survival was certainly not expected. Several other Reference Group members also suggested that superintendents themselves contribute to their short tenures—but for different reasons.

> For the ones who are still trying to operate districts in an autocratic way, I think that they're going to continue to have short tenures. Eventually that leadership style will be eliminated because communities are now understanding that you can't change superintendents year in and year out.

> In some instances people are interested in those [urban] superintendencies because of status, because of power, and because of the dollars that go with it. They are not really willing to make those decisions and stay on track of why urban schools exist.

> I just believe the wishy-washiness of superintendents gets them into more trouble than if they were to take a stand. But not take a stand that's going to be self-serving to them but does come along to clearly show I'm here to do what's best for the students. Do that and I think you can survive. Urban superintendents can survive much longer than what they have.

The conclusion that many large-district superintendents leave their positions because of board changes was reinforced by another superintendent when he speculated about the rapid turnover of superintendents in districts making up the Council of Great City Schools.

> I think it may be linked to the quality of school board members elected in the last few years. I think we have had a shift in the kind of person who either runs for the board or seeks appointment to a school board. They come with agendas of their own rather than accepting the roles outlined in the statutes. That may not be a very clear answer. It is awfully frustrating to spend an inordinate amount of time with new school board members to convince them that what you have been doing the last few years has been in the best interests of the school district. Too many of the new board members want to turn back from recent decisions.

When discussing the issue of turnover, several of the Reference Group members emphasized the importance of maintaining a degree of independence. One explained that his personal survival had never been a source of anxiety because he had been eligible for retirement before he took the job.

> I think my position is unique. Most of the superintendents I know are hired from outside the school system or are insiders who are 45 to 50 years old. When they run out of their 2 to 5 years, they pack up and move to a new job or they assume some lower position in the district. My situation is unique because I was eligible for retirement 12 years ago. I never really worried about what I was going to do next. And so everything that has happened to me since becoming superintendent has only required my own mental adjustment to the situation. If they fired me, they would just shove me into happiness. I never had to deal with a board that was out to get rid of me or a board that was thinking that my time was up. I've been real lucky. So perhaps many things others have to deal with just haven't been part of my agenda.

Yet another superintendent added to the long list of potential reasons for the short tenure of their peers.

> I don't have a lot of optimism about the urban superintendency becoming any less complex or any easier. I think it will become more difficult unless there is some kind of a change in the support from the general community, community leaders, and boards of education. It's such a difficult job that I think few people are going to be able to tolerate the complexities of the job for very long.

One of the superintendents discussed his longevity in the context of his self-perceptions of practice:

> I think I have—in spite of the fact that it's a very political position—I've kept foremost in all the decisions that I need to make—I've tried to answer the question, Is it good for students? And so the whole "students come first" belief system has been behind everything that I've done. So I haven't got caught in political problems that some of my colleagues have.

Compensation

Many observers conclude that administrators have been lured to the urban superintendency by huge salaries and fringe benefits. In 1959, for instance, superintendents in communities with over 500,000 population had a median salary of $25,000—over twice the median salary for all school superintendents in that year (Knezevich, 1962). But do urban superintendencies continue to offer the highest salaries in public elementary and secondary education? The answer is both "yes" and "no."

During the 1985-86 school year, superintendents in districts having membership in the Council of Great City Schools reported an average salary of $80,106 (Council of Great City Schools, 1986). In his 1990 study, Ornstein (1992) found that superintendents in districts

TABLE 3.1 Annual Salary Data for the Reference Group for
School Year 1992-93 (N = 17)

Range	Number Reporting	Percentage of Group
$90,000-99,999	3	17.7
$100,000-109,999	3	17.7
$110,000-119,999	2	11.8
$120,000-129,999	5	29.4
$130,000-139,999	0	0.0
$140,000-149,999	2	11.7
$150,000-159,000	1	5.8
$160,000+	1	5.8

NOTE: Group low = $90,704; group high = $195,000; actual group mean = $114,760.

with 33,500 or more students had average salaries of just over $100,000. Slightly over one in three had a six-figure salary.

Data collected from the Reference Group in 1993 suggested that the average salary for large-district superintendents is continuing to rise. The mean for this group was approximately $115,000—about $35,000 higher than the 1985-1986 figure reported by the Council of Great City Schools and $15,000 higher than that reported by Ornstein in 1992. Annual salary data for the 1993 Reference Group are presented in Table 3.1. Since 1985 to 1986, the average salary of superintendents in these urban districts has increased about $4,338 per year.

Reference Group members also were asked to provide information relative to their total compensation packages (i.e., the total dollar value of salary plus fringe benefits). Only 12 of the 17 provided this information. The lowest reported annual value was $110,000, the highest was $230,000, and the average (mean) was $154,000. These figures are displayed in Table 3.2.

There is little question that superintendents in the nation's largest school districts receive compensation packages that appear high when compared to those of superintendents in rural or small-town school districts; but they are not really high when compared to superintendent salaries in affluent suburban districts. In suburban New York and Chicago, for instance, some superintendents in districts with fewer than

TABLE 3.2 Dollar Value of Reference Group Annual
Compensation Package (*N* = 12)

Range *(Total Value of Compensation)*	*Number Reporting*
$110,000-119,999	2
$120,000-129,999	2
$130,000-139,999	1
$140,000-149,999	1
$150,000-159,000	1
$160,000-169,000	2
$170,000-179,000	0
$180,000+	3

8,000 students had compensation packages that exceeded $150,000 during the 1992-93 school year. A national study of 450 superintendents in school districts with student enrollment of 15,000 or more during the 1991-92 school year yielded a mean base salary of $97,694, a figure that represented a 3.3% increase over the previous year. Thirty-nine percent of the superintendents in this group reported base compensation in excess of $100,000 (McCord & Kops, 1992). But beyond the impressions that may be drawn from average salaries, the fact remains that the very highest salaries paid to school executives continue to be found in the nation's gigantic school districts, such as New York and Los Angeles.

In many suburban school systems, superintendents have broken through the magic $100,000 mark. Ultimately, this fact will influence big-city salaries, driving them upward. But urban school boards frequently are caught between the realities of the job market and conservative inclinations of taxpayers. Thus there is a tendency to structure compensation packages so that an increasing portion of the remuneration is placed in nonsalary items (e.g., tax shelters, retirement programs).

Final Thoughts on Job Conditions

This chapter has looked at the declining tenure of urban superintendents and its potential causes. The revolving door to the superintendent's office has negative consequences for both the organization and the person. If anything, school reform efforts have brought to light the futility of trying to restructure schools without leadership stability; the brief window of opportunity accorded superintendents has done nothing to move them more toward the role of instructional leader. And despite the high insecurity of their jobs, urban superintendents are typically expected to be loyal to their school boards, city officials, and school district.

The limited tenure of urban superintendents is blamed on a myriad of factors. Some in the position say that many of their peers are concerned solely with their own careers, and that they consequently fail to make a commitment to their employer. Others blame social conditions, citing crime, violence, and poverty as the reasons that far too many children are at risk of not succeeding in the public schools. Still others say that school boards are to blame. Rather than earnestly pursuing school improvement, they march a new administrator before the public every few years to present the illusion of change. In reality, the reasons probably vary from city to city, and they are likely to be an intricate mix of circumstances rather than any one factor.

Salaries paid to many of these leaders raise eyebrows, especially among those who believe that all public employees ought to be "servants." In truth, many big-cities pay their superintendents less than they would receive if they were working in an affluent suburb. Yet the highest paid of all superintendents are still found in the major metropolitan areas.

FOUR

SCHOOL BOARDS

Partners or Adversaries?

Boards and superintendents inevitably face the same type of dilemmas, and frequently are caught between the same cross-pressures.

—Stephen J. Knezevich

Although elementary and secondary education has been under intense scrutiny since the early 1980s, only in the past few years has the focus of school reform broadened to include issues of governance. The present system of local control, a system through which states delegate authority to elected or appointed school boards, has changed very little since the early 20th century (Danzberger & Usdan, 1994). In part, failed attempts to improve schools through intensification mandates have revealed the importance of policy and politics at the school district level. Reformers now generally agree that meaningful change is more likely if it is pursued at the micro level (school or school district) and predicated on goals that are supported by the community, school board, and employees.

Given current governance problems in large-city school districts, it is difficult to imagine that less than two decades ago, a study of urban superintendent perceptions found that 80% of these administrators gave their school boards an "A" or "B" rating (Cawelti, 1982).

As shown in this chapter, it is doubtful that this finding would be replicated today. Perhaps more than any other factor, conflict produced by dwindling resources and increased demands for services has heightened tensions between school boards and administrators. Each crisis takes its toll, political behavior becomes more overt, and relationships suffer (Todras, 1993). Public demands for change place all school officials in a defensive posture, and as these demands intensify, the relationships between boards and superintendents become more critical.

Growing Uncertainty of Relationships

Textbooks describe school boards as legal entities that have authority only when members act as a group in accordance with state constitutions. In the real world of practice, however, superintendents readily recognize that boards are five or seven or more distinct individuals—each behaving on the basis of personal beliefs, interests, or causes. Often in big cities, these individual goals are tied to special-interest groups or neighborhood coalitions that help to get a board member elected or appointed.

Because it is likely that modern urban board members have multiple and diverse agendas, superintendents usually find it in their best interest to establish positive one-to-one relationships with as many of the board members as possible. Blumberg (1985) observed that "both the superintendent's professional reputation and his personal welfare depend greatly on his ability to influence its [school board] decisions. Further, it is primarily through the one-to-one linkage between superintendent and school board member that attempts to influence take place" (p. 76). More specifically, a superintendent's power, in general and with the school board, is dependent on personal ties, loyalties, interpersonal relationships, and persuasive communication skills (Crowson, 1987). But when school board members dislike each other, or when they represent opposing views on major policy issues, the task of establishing positive relationships with all board members becomes much more difficult.

More often than not, today's urban school board consists of individuals who are a rather diverse group—not only philosophically but behaviorally. Studying board members in six different districts, Tallerico (1989) found that their behavioral inclinations ranged from passive acquiescence to proactive supportiveness to restive vigilance. As a consequence, their frames of decision making are also variegated. For example, whereas some function largely in a political world where compromise and special interests dominate, others weigh information in relation to community interests. These different dispositions contribute to expectations for the superintendent that almost ensure some degree of inter-role conflict.

Another discomforting aspect of the superintendency is the reality that power stemming from positive relationships with individual board members can dissipate rather quickly. A positive relationship with a school board member may take several years to cultivate, but it can be ruined by a single incident of conflict. Because of this reality, superintendents often feel like they are walking on eggshells when they are around board members. A misconstrued comment, the failure to accommodate the request for a favor, or the unwillingness to support a particular position on a controversial policy matter may be all that is needed to initiate an adversarial relationship. Even more frustrating, superintendents live with the reality that regardless of how positive their personal relationships with board members may be, this advantage can be eradicated by a single school board election or mayor's appointment. There is never any assurance that a staunch supporter will not be replaced by an avowed enemy. This is one of the primary reasons that instability on a school board usually spells trouble for the superintendent.

Conflicting Demands Magnified in Urban Settings

Those who study public schools have realized for some time that school board members are often caught between two conflicting role expectations. On the one hand, national and state associations provide expectations in codes of ethics that urge them to refrain from interference in the day-to-day operations of schools and to avoid acting in an individual capacity. Essentially, these expectations are built around a preferred relationship between boards and superintendents that respects the professionalism of the administrative and teaching staff. In contrast, taxpayers usually view board members in a political context: They want them to intervene on their behalf and take care of their problems. In essence, they want board members to behave like elected city officials.

Conflict generated by the interface of professionalism and politics remains pervasive in public education. In many communities, school board members refuse to honor an elusive line that separates policy from administration (Trotter & Downey, 1989), and as a result, they are constantly having to choose between what they see as their ideal and real roles. This problem is magnified in urban settings, where we often find fragmented boards whose members are aligned with neighborhoods, ethic/racial groups, special interests, or focused initiatives.

Studying school board member behavior in New Jersey, Greene (1990) concluded that citizens often had little chance to raise their concerns at public meetings. He claimed that such sessions were typically dominated by the administrators and guided by a set agenda. Accordingly, many citizens who had problems, special requests, or questions turned to board members with the expectation that they would be responsive. When asked whether they followed a political or professional role, answers from school board members in this study were contradictory. This suggested that many of them were attempting to deal with role conflict by compromising. Findings also revealed that the extent of board member political activity was influenced by certain variables such as electoral competition in school board races, the complexity of the school district, and the reelection plans of board members.

In summary, the life of urban school board members is made more difficult by expectations that they wear two very different hats. Although this conflict is not a recent development, it certainly has been made worse by several conditions. Foremost are increasing demands for services, dwindling resources, and the failure of school districts to adapt more democratic procedures for citizen input.

Sources of Friction Between
Superintendents and School Boards

Common sense suggests that harmony between superintendents and school boards is most likely when the two parties operate with similar decision-making styles. Katz (1993), for instance, suggested that the most productive matches occurred (a) between high corporate-type boards (i.e., boards that thrive on data and formality and express commitment to standards and excellence rather than the community) and task-oriented superintendents and (b) between familial-type boards (i.e., boards that thrive on informality and oral communication and show extreme loyalty to the community) and relationship-oriented superintendents. But in large cities today, school boards do not fit neatly into either of these packages; they are extremely complex entities made up of factions and individual crusaders. Some board members display neither a corporate nor a familial orientation; rather they function largely as political activists, advocates for pressure groups, or seekers of higher office.

Expectedly, one of the most common sources of friction between school board members and superintendents is the differing values and beliefs of their respective roles. As noted, the textbook division of policy making and policy implementation is not universally accepted, and it is particularly challenged in large cities. Former Cleveland superintendent Alfred Tutela observed that board members are constantly looking for ways to gain favor with voters, and often this encourages them to infringe on administrative activities. This may even include dictating decisions on contracts and job appointments. According to him, the superintendent who resists these interventions into administrative turf is headed for trouble (Rist, 1990).

Recounting how a new school board spelled the beginning of the end of his reign as chancellor of the New York City schools, Joseph Fernandez attributed much of his difficulties to working with a seven-member board that included five new appointees. He grew increasingly frustrated by what he believed was a breach of the imaginary line that should divide the authority of a school board and the authority of a superintendent. Although he had experienced such infringements in his previous job in Miami, he judged the new board members in New York to be less sophisticated. He felt that they showed little respect for the demarcation between administration and policy making. He claimed that they cared about neither masking their intentions nor accepting responsibility for protecting the integrity of his office. Their posturing before television cameras, their demands for information, and the lack of control exercised by the school board president convinced him he was in a "bad marriage" (Fernandez & Underwood, 1993, p. 238). Fernandez was the fourth new superintendent the district had in 4 years, and after just 3 years in office, he found himself working for a board substantially different than the one that had hired him.

Concerns such as those voiced by the former New York City school chancellor are congruent with data that were reported in a study sponsored by the National School Boards Association. Summarizing the findings, McCurdy and Hymes (1992) listed factors identified by urban school board members and superintendents as responsible for destabilizing their relationships. Four were commonly identified by both groups:

- Board members often do not understand the differences between their roles and those of superintendents.
- Poor communication by both parties contributes to conflict.
- Board members often enter office with personal agendas.
- Board members and superintendents often fail to establish a necessary level of mutual trust.

McCloud and McKenzie (1994) categorized factors that they found affected superintendent and board relations in urban schools into two broad groups: external and internal. In the former, they included demands for reform, policy issues from religious and other special-interest groups, interventions from city government, heightened expectations for collaboration, and long-standing social issues such as desegregation. In the latter, they listed board members who had a single-issue agenda and factionalism on the board itself.

Perhaps the most prevalent contemporary criticism of urban school board members relates to political activity. As he was leaving his position as superintendent of the St. Paul school district, David Bennett (1991) pulled few punches when he asserted that the types of individuals serving on urban school boards were changing. He labeled the new breed "pure politicians" and described them as follows: "This kind of board member does not evidence any special interest in education above and beyond elected service in any political office. This board member behaves like any other political office holder, concerned primarily with reelection or higher political office and paying assiduous attention to serving political constituents" (p. 23).

It would be foolish to suggest that there are one or two reasons why superintendents get into trouble with their school boards. There are many, and some are the result of inappropriate behavior by the administrators. In general, however, tensions erupt when factionalism on the board leads to diverse expectations regarding behavior of superintendents and the positions that they should take. In large cities, turnover on school boards is becoming more frequent, and this often raises the probability of factionalism.

Reference Group Perceptions of School Boards

Conflict between urban superintendents and their school board members has received a significant amount of attention in the media over the past decade. As such, I expected members of the Reference Group to be generally negative when they described their relationships with board members. But when they rated their school board members on a 5-point continuum ranging from 1 = *never supportive* to 5 = *always supportive,* 41% gave a rating of 4 (toward *always supportive*), 12% gave a rating of 5 (*always supportive*), 42% gave a neutral rating of 3, and only one gave a rating of 2 (toward *never supportive*). These results are especially interesting in light of the fact that about half of the Reference Group left their jobs within 1 year after supplying information.

Reference Group members also were asked if they thought that urban school board members were more political than board members in other types of districts. Slightly fewer than half of them believed that they were more political, and the remainder said they were uncertain—but none said that they were less political. In part, this outcome may be due to the fact that a number of the superintendents had not been administrators in nonurban districts.

Asked if he agreed that many urban board members were pure politicians, one superintendent in the Reference Group answered, "Definitely." He saw a number of individuals using their positions on the school board as a stepping stone to higher elected office.

The person who chaired the board that selected me is a county commissioner. She used the school board position as a springboard to that position. The second most active board member just ran for mayor. They are looking for something either at the state level or for national appointments. So I'm not sure that there are many who think they are of the quality to receive a national appointment—but a few have been able to get them. At least the thought runs through their minds— and their actions are geared toward getting recognition for the purpose of personal advancement.

Another of the superintendents responded to my question with a similar perspective.

As I have observed boards over the years, I find that they have two reasons for getting on school boards. One is genuinely being interested in the schools and believing that they could help shape the future. The other was that school board membership was being used as a stepping stone for something else. What I have found is that board members are easily subjected to political influence, especially from other political leaders at the community, state, and national levels. They will at times let that political sense override their best judgment in terms of decision making. For some, being on the school board is primarily a political effort.

When asked whether the current form of governance (i.e., school boards) remains effective for urban districts, the Reference Group showed substantial division. The results were "definitely yes," 17.6%; "probably yes," 23.5%; "probably no," 35.3%; "definitely no," 11.8%; and "undecided," 11.8%. One superintendent explained during an interview that the current structure of governance almost encourages individual board members to challenge aspects of the superintendent's agenda. School boards often employ superintendents because of their visions, but when the goals are separated and isolated, some board members find themselves opposing the superintendent. Several of the superintendents commented that it becomes extremely difficult for them to execute a long-range plan without alienating some board members.

Suggested Remedies

A report issued by the Council of Urban Boards of Education in 1992 noted that superintendents and board members possess an awareness of their relationship problems. This document identified the major destabilizing factors as confusion among board members as to their roles, poor communication between the superintendent and board members, and personal agendas that conflicted with organizational initiatives (McCloud & McKenzie, 1994). Clearly, the problems that exist between superintendents and boards are recognized and have been accurately categorized, but these accomplishments have done little to change behavior.

As far back as the mid-1980s, some critics were declaring that school boards had outlived their usefulness in big cities. Viteritti (1986), for example, argued that true decentralization would be more likely if both school boards and the superintendency were eradicated. He suggested that schools would be more responsive if they were run by an appointed commissioner of education, a person who would be appointed by the mayor and serve as part of the mayor's administration. In his view, this arrangement would make the schools more responsive to the special needs of neighborhoods in large metropolitan areas. This exemplifies the classic political perspective of school administration.

Another perspective that moves away from the long-standing notion of professional control in public education urges school board members to become more active in school operations. Critics who embrace this position argue that school reform will not be successful unless board members immerse themselves in critical issues. Jean Zlotkin (1993), a practicing attorney and school board member in California, is one who has publicly taken this stand. She believes that trustees must become leaders and superintendents must become facilitators. She wrote,

> Traditionally, few boards ever have meetings without the superintendent physically present; they are much like children relying on a parent—or students relying on a teacher. Just as we see the kids in a classroom, when excellence is not demanded, when thoughtfulness is not valued, and when self-directed

meaningful work is not required, then apathy and medioc-
rity result. (p. 24)

Jacqueline Danzberger (1994), who has written extensively on
the topics of urban schools and school boards, agreed that governance problems are serious but suggested a less drastic solution. Needed
school restructuring would not occur, in her opinion, unless boards
themselves were reshaped. She felt that the public was using the
schools to address a range of political demands, and that this condition had led to fragmentation and directed attention away from institutional planning. She argued that without reaching consensus on
such fundamental issues as the role of school boards and the purposes of education, boards would "focus on short-term micromanagement of the school system and . . . respond to special interests,
factions, and specific complaints of constituents" (p. 371). She called
for state government to rewrite laws and regulations that would direct and restrict school board activity to ensure proper planning and
interactions with the community.

Mounting tensions between urban superintendents and their boards
indicate that the desired stability is not likely unless the role and
functions of school boards are reexamined. It is virtually impossible
for a group of policy makers to act in the best interests of society if
they are constantly responding to isolated problems and interests. In
a growing number of cities, issues that divide the public, such as sex
education and outcome-based education, are becoming the platforms
for school board candidates. And it is not uncommon for factions
representing both sides of these issues to get one or more candidates
elected.

Final Thoughts

Personal relationships with school board members have always
been critical to superintendents. Leadership—that is, the ability to
move people and resources toward desired goals—requires power.
Regardless of whether administrators pursue this power professionally, politically, or through a combination of the two means, their

efforts are less likely to be fruitful in situations in which the board is fractionalized and constantly changing.

Problems between school board members and superintendents are frequently cited as a cause of inertia in public education. More correctly, they are symptomatic of the real causes. Many current reform initiatives have brought to light the difficulties of trying to make schools more responsive and democratic while promoting professionalism for teachers and administrators. Both school board members and superintendents have become mired in role conflict, and neither faces the prospect of long terms in office.

FIVE

POLITICS

The Center of Activity

Conflict is the DNA of the superintendency.
—Larry Cuban

When he wrote his classic study of three prominent big-city superintendents in the mid-1970s, Cuban (1976) noted that far more information was known about the salaries of urban superintendents than about the actual nature of their jobs. There continue to be many unanswered questions, especially those that relate to the political behavior of superintendents themselves. For example, do urban superintendents see their jobs as being largely political? How do they describe the intensity of political activity around them?

The Political Nature of the Superintendency

Even though many insightful observers have concluded that common sense and savvy were always necessary survival traits for superintendents, there is growing evidence that the political nature of the job has become more intense in recent years. In large measure, early urban superintendents succeeded in casting themselves as professionals, and thus above petty politics. But their accomplishment is best described as an accommodation rather than a victory of public conviction. Tensions revolving around the question of whether professionals, politically elected officials, or the community as a whole should control public schools have not been eased.

Underlying professionalism is the contention that administrators possess special knowledge and skills not held by the public. In many respects, this position is legitimized in every state by licensing and certification requirements. But in reality, the notion that administrators are true professionals has always been contested. This has been visible not only in conflict with the public, but also in strife with teachers. Collective bargaining and unionism often have challenged the right and wisdom of allowing a few people to make critical decisions on behalf of children and the entire community.

Some historians (e.g., Spring, 1985) refer to two political frames in the work environments of school administrators, the traditional and the emerging. In the former are issues involving scarce resources and competing needs (this is the conventional definition of politics). In the latter are the realities of diminishing control (due largely to legal and legislative interventions) and altered power structures. In the early decades of the 20th century, big-city superintendents worked with school board members who represented the white middle class of America. Not only were school board members apt to think alike, but superintendents were often appointed to office because their values and beliefs mirrored those of board members. But more recently in large cities,

> monopolistic power structures have changed and are being replaced by ones based on democratic pluralism, in which there are ideological splits between liberals and conservatives, as well as pressures from organized minority groups and community groups lobbying for special programs. In addition, teacher unionization and organized student-rights groups have made it difficult for superintendents to deal in areas where they have traditionally controlled. (Spring, 1985, p. 151)

In essence, big-city superintendents have two choices when they work with fractionalized school boards: They can attempt to align with one faction, or they can attempt to remain neutral. Neither option guarantees survival. Public administration requires superintendents to gain the cooperation of others; yet they feel they must operate the schools professionally or their power will be eroded even more (Dahl, 1969). For many, there is a constant internal struggle regarding compromise, and this strife has legal, professional, and moral/ethical dimensions that often are at odds with political expediency.

From the earliest days of urban districts, many superintendents have shown ambivalence toward accepting a negotiator-statesman role. Although they recognized that their ability to function effectively in a political arena was necessary, they often went to great lengths to convince their publics that they were not politicians. Cuban (1985) referred to this condition when he wrote:

> Because of the professional taboos, superintendents keep the exercise of political skills a secret art, practiced quietly and covertly. Nonetheless, among superintendents (and informed observers), any chief who survives a series of changes in school board membership wins automatic nomination to the survivor's hall of fame. Thus, the measure of a superintendent's political skill—but not necessarily of his or her leadership— is survival for a decade or longer in one locale. (p. 29)

By classifying themselves as professionals, superintendents sought protection from partisan pressures that permeated the work of other public officials. And although this strategy was partially effective, it never provided complete protection from periodic episodes of intense conflict involving tensions between politics and professionalism. At best, the cloak of professionalism was moderately successful in removing public education from direct involvement in partisan politics. Although the urban school bureaucracy never became apolitical, it did evolve as an independent force competing for power and resources within big-city government (Cronin, 1973).

Studying four women who had recently exited the urban superintendency, Tallerico, Poole, and Burstyn (1994) found that these individuals almost always used the term *politics* negatively when talking about their administrative experiences. Even more revealing was their tendency to view the term *political* as oppositional to *educational*.

Historically, efforts to professionalize school administration have been largely responsible for casting political behavior as the antithesis of professional behavior.

Two other relatively recent developments have also served to intensify the political nature of the superintendency. School reform has brought new players into the policy arena, and because there are more cooks in the kitchen, big-city administrators have been bombarded with recommendations from business, political, and community power brokers. Second, friction between teachers and administrators regarding the sharing of power and authority has been augmented by concepts such as site-based management and teacher empowerment. In essence, professionalism has not only two time-related frames but also two group-related dimensions. One entails conflict with the community (and its leaders) over control; the other includes conflict with teachers about alignment within the education profession.

Even board members do not especially like to talk about the need for superintendents to be skilled politicians. Jonathan Wilson (1991), who served three terms as the chair of the National School Boards Association's Council of Urban Boards of Education while serving as a board member in Des Moines, Iowa, authored an article detailing what urban school boards expect in a superintendent. He declared that superintendents who possessed the following traits could feel some confidence in succeeding in the urban superintendency: an ability to inspire, business savvy, sensitivity to diversity, self-confidence, sensitivity to board members, high energy, and a sense of humor. The sole mention of potential conflict came under the topic of the superintendent's ability to inspire. The author suggested that a superintendent with a strong vision could prevent conflict, and he warned, "But if the vision is weak, board members and citizens with competing agendas will step in, and conflict will inevitably result" (p. 32).

Reference Group Perceptions

Both the media and professional literature have described the depth of political activity currently found in urban school districts. Responses from the Reference Group certainly verify this message. When asked about political activity in their jobs, 77% of respondents classified it as "definitely hardball," and the remainder said it was somewhat that way.

Commenting on the political nature of his job, one superintendent in the Reference Group alluded to the tension between professionalism and politics. This individual suggested that vision and endurance were essential in contemporary practice despite the overwhelming level of conflict and subsequent invitations to compromise:

> It is political hardball. And I think sometimes that you have to go to the game understanding that it's hardball, but still having a vision or direction for what you want to accomplish. And if it means that you strike out, you can't worry about that. You have to keep your eye on your target.

Another superintendent alluded to the traditional and emerging political frames of his work:

> Well, it's hardball because you're getting hit from so many different angles. And people come at you because they have set agendas that they're pushing.

As noted earlier, contemporary urban superintendents are not naive—they recognize that intense political behavior is inherent in their jobs. In conducting my research, I found the superintendents to be most candid when commenting on the political nature of their responsibilities. Citing a particular incident, a superintendent summarized how the mayor in his city had used the school district's budget as an excuse for not giving city employees a salary increase. Employing the popular tactic of declaring himself to be the "taxpayers' friend and watchdog," the mayor told the city council that a lack of fiscal control on the part of school officials (the district had just advertised a budget increase for the coming year) prevented him from recommending increases in the city budget. He noted that to do so would place additional burdens on citizens who were already being overtaxed. In addition, the mayor insinuated that the superintendent was "owned" by the districts' employee unions. "Now," the superintendent told me, "that's political hardball!"

Another superintendent pointed to problems with big-city government officials when he described the prevalence of political activity in his job:

> I have my own problems with the mayor, who I think wants to have a lot more to say about what happens in the schools. This is not a system where the mayor appoints the school board. So he does it through his bully pulpit as mayor. You're always engaged in some political thing out there. But to me, that is the nature of the job. That's what I think this job is. These jobs are so difficult, they require a lot of different skills in order to, first off, survive personally, but also to move any kind of agenda forward. You've got to know politics. You've got to be able to deal in public relations. You clearly have to know something about education and organizational behavior. You obviously have to have some verbal skills and analytical skills—and then you put the whole political thing on top of that. It's a daunting task!

Yet another superintendent indicated that while politics were certainly visible in his work, the nature of such activities in his school district had become less vicious. He attributed the change to improved communications.

> At one time, you could not get the city council, school board, and state representatives in the same room because we had such an adversarial relationship. It was sort of "standoffish." Every one was attacking public education. But we had a dinner one night, sponsored by the school district, and I convinced the board to invite our state representatives and our local elected officials so we could all discuss education. This gave us a chance to explain to them what we were trying to do in the schools. What I found out is that once people understand your mission, you get better cooperation. These individuals rallied around the school district to support our tax levy—even the ones who were running for reelection. Things are really moving well here, and we raised $370,000

to support our tax election. The community came together because they saw a need, and they bought into my philosophy of education.

Blending State and Local Politics

Although not specifically mentioned by any of the superintendents in this study, the blending of state-house politics and big-city politics has emerged as another factor affecting the political lives of urban leaders. Pipho (1988) noted that problems in urban school districts, such as a lack of student productivity in Chicago and the deteriorated state of school facilities in New York City, were increasingly attracting the attention of state legislatures. Two conclusions on the part of state officials appear to be primarily responsible for their interventions: (a) They see some urban districts as being incapable of solving their own problems, and (b) they see the problems of these districts reaching a level of severity at which they threaten the welfare of the state as a whole. Regardless of how well-meaning or necessary such intrusions may be, they unavoidably contribute to public perceptions that local school officials are incapable of managing their institutions.

In the next 10 years or so, actions by state legislatures and governors are likely to reshape the operations and structure of urban school districts. A lack of measurable improvement in student performance, rising crime and violence, deteriorating facilities, voter cries for change, and the legal reality that state government is ultimately responsible for public education are converging to force action. If ideas such as choice, site-based management, teacher empowerment, charter schools, and privatization fail to deliver their intended outcomes, state officials are apt to take the drastic step of dissolving urban districts. They may either carve these districts into small pieces—each becoming a separate school system—or they may opt to redistribute territories among existing suburban districts. Potential extinction is rapidly becoming the greatest political reality of the urban superintendency.

Final Thoughts on Politics

Responses I received from the Reference Group indicated that politics are pervasive in urban school administration. Competition for scarce resources, demands for change, continuing uncertainty about the control of public education, and rival reform agendas are but some of the variables that generate intense conflict that can overpower the political skills of even the best educated and most experienced superintendents. Survival often depends on one's ability to align with the proper faction or to maintain neutrality without alienating those possessing power. In a story printed in the *New York Times* in February 1993 (Celis, 1993), Frank Petruzielo, superintendent of the Houston Independent School District (the fifth largest in the nation) was quoted as saying that politics absolutely played a big role in the superintendency. He indicated that competency often was not the issue, and that it was the political pressure that made the superintendency more demanding than comparable jobs in private industry.

Although at first glance, urban school districts certainly look like classic bureaucracies (authority is centralized and policy is made by relatively few), they are unique institutions in which the primary group of employees (teachers) is relatively unsupervised (Oxley, 1994) and the legitimate and professional power of administrators is constantly being contested. Given the turmoil and intensity of community-based problems, many urban districts have a precarious future. Consequently each new reform-related idea constitutes a threat—to the organizational design of school districts, to the governance structure of school boards, and to the legitimate power and authority of administrators.

S I X

DECISION-MAKING INFLUENCES

*Regardless of the focus or substance, a seemingly absolute
condition of the superintendency is that there are only rarely
days when the superintendent is not called upon to make a
decision that will create some conflict, or is not involved
somehow in conflicts of his own making.*

−Arthur Blumberg

T he extent of any superintendent's personal power is conditioned
by a multitude of community, organizational, and personal variables.
As a result, the decision-making behavior of top executives is non-
standard across school districts. But even in situations in which power
is quite limited, the superintendent is likely to make a number of
decisions required by day-to-day operations. The legitimate responsibilities of the position require action—even if that action is to rele-
gate problems to others. In this respect, it is important to differentiate
decisions from power. School boards, for example, possess the authority
to set policy. The fact that superintendents do not have that power
does not mean they do not make decisions that affect outcomes. They
determine what data will be given to the board members; they establish a process and timetable for deliberation; they formulate the recommendation that goes to the school board.

Writing about administrative behavior, Boyan (1988) broadly categorized potential decision-making influences as personal and situ-

ational (the latter including both intraorganizational and extraorganizational subcategories). He noted that most research on the decision-making behavior of superintendents has focused on only one of the categories or subcategories; far less attention has been given to integrative studies (research that simultaneously examines personal and situational variables). As a consequence, the literature provides only fragments of information about this important element of practice.

Rational and Political Decision Making

As noted in Chapter 2, Cuban (1976) approached the issue of leadership style in his study of three urban superintendents in the 1970s by employing constructs that summarized three distinct roles— negotiator-statesman, administrative chief, and teacher-scholar—and focusing on superintendents' ability to make transitions among these roles to meet varying expectations. He discovered that the leaders relied upon tried and true methods even though environmental and organizational circumstances surrounding their work had changed significantly. When their actions proved to be unsuccessful, the three superintendents believed they had approached the challenges properly. Rather than seeing that they had become victims of their own experiences, previous successes, and inflexibility, they attributed their difficulties to the fact that others had changed the rules and neglected to tell them.

Even though distinctions can be made between leadership style and decision making, it is clear that the two are highly related. Research on practice suggests that success or failure is often affected by the administrator's ability to make adjustments to prevailing conditions in the school district and community (Boyan, 1988). Individuals who successfully make transitions among their many role expectations and who possess a professional knowledge base that allows them to make appropriate decisions when wearing different hats are more likely to be successful than those who lack these qualities. These role transitions almost always include modifications in decision-making behavior.

In large institutions with centralized authority, rational approaches to management continue to be embraced by many executives. Observations of the restructuring efforts of profit-seeking companies provide excellent examples of this condition and its ultimate impact on organizational development. Faced with global competition and the accompanying need to be more sensitive to consumer needs and wants, giant corporations often found that the highest barrier in the path to new cultures and climates was managerial behavior. Managers in these companies reacted to conflict by attempting minor adjustments rather than major structural changes (Lasher, 1990). Because of their training and socialization, these individuals were not encouraged to seek optimal alternatives; rather managers often learn to make decisions by selecting a response from a list of satisfactory options (March & Simon, 1958). New goals, new slogans, and even financial incentives usually proved to be insufficient to alter their behavior. Eventually, top executives realized that a paradigm shift, one that concentrated on educating rather than training managers, was needed. The intent was to move managers from convictions that employee behavior was rational and predictable to a position that encouraged them to use analytical and critical thinking skills in making decisions. In other words, their jobs became less routine.

If administrative behavior is difficult to change in organizations that operate in highly competitive markets, it is far more difficult in public schools—institutions that have had only token competition. The continued existence of public education is taken for granted in this country, and reward structures for employees are dissimilar to those commonly found in business. Historically, school administrators have been socialized to avoid failure rather than to take risks. This behavior is reinforced by reward structures that relate to schools as institutions of stability. Even when failure occurs, it may be rewarded rather than punished (Boaz, 1991). Far too often, administrator decisions are judged in the context of political positions held by influential others, not by school improvement and student outcomes. Studies of attempted reforms in big-city school systems during the 1980s, for instance, often reveal how state and local politics takes precedence over professional knowledge in key decisions (e.g., Pink, 1992).

Because most superintendents are in office for such a brief time, it is virtually impossible to accurately determine the value of their contributions. They often are bombarded with emergencies and distracted from pursuing long-range goals. They learn from experience that they will be held more accountable for managing resources and settling disputes than for attempting long-term educational initiatives.

Behavior of Contemporary Practitioners

Are contemporary superintendents behaving any differently as a result of demands for teacher empowerment, community empowerment, and decentralization? Has the school reform movement reduced expectations of rationality or the influence of politics? These questions were on my mind when I asked the Reference Group about their decision-making procedures and the factors that most influenced their decisions. More specifically, I asked them to identify the extent to which 10 common factors affected their decisions, by having them specify a point on a continuum ranging from *most influential* to *no influence* for each of the 10 factors. The outcomes for this part of the study are presented in Table 6.1.

The results fail to show clear distinctions between the professional and political arenas of decision making. Three of the items, "educational theories and research," "input from administrative staff," and "input from teachers," are associated more directly with professional decision making than are the others. "Personal beliefs" can relate to both political and professional considerations; the remaining variables are skewed toward local political conditions. All of the factors appear to play some part in influencing behavior, and the results indicate that superintendents continue to juggle professional and political considerations.

The top executive in a large organization is typically expected to possess knowledge and skills that are greater than those possessed by his or her subordinates. This belief is manifested by the fact that this individual is granted a great deal of power and authority and access to information not readily available to others. Superintendents are also affected by the pragmatic consideration that they will be held personally responsible for major decisions. Collectively, these factors prompt superintendents to have a great deal of faith in their own convictions.

Further insights about decision making were obtained in interviews with Reference Group members. During these conversations,

TABLE 6.1 The Relative Importance of Factors Affecting Decision
Making

Factor	Level of Influence			
(Percentage of Total Responses)	Most	.	.	.	None
Fiscal resources	70.6	23.5	5.9	0	0
Personal beliefs	29.4	70.6	0	0	0
Educational theories and research	11.8	58.8	29.4	0	0
Input from administrative staff	11.8	58.8	29.4	0	0
Environmental socioeconomic conditions	11.8	41.2	41.2	5.9	0
School board member positions/opinions	5.9	47.1	41.2	5.9	0
Input from teachers	0	47.1	47.1	5.9	0
Environmental political conditions	0	35.3	58.8	5.9	0
Teacher union positions/ pressure	0	29.4	47.1	23.5	0
Concerns for personal survival	0	17.6	29.4	41.2	11.8

I was struck by recurring comments that ideas and initiatives would be
evaluated largely by two criteria—efficiency and political acceptance.
Consider the following comments made by a superintendent discussing
decisions he had made regarding enrollment problems.

> I decided that year-round education was one way to control
> some of the growth in our school system. I put together a task
> force and spent about a year getting the community to buy
> into this solution. We thought we could save about $80 mil-
> lion by getting into year-round education in our elementary
> schools. The board was well aware of what we were doing;
> and after we spent about a year studying the issue, I picked
> approximately 28 schools where I thought year-round edu-
> cation would alleviate overcrowding. Plus the fact that since
> becoming superintendent, I have worked hard to get year-
> round education not just to relieve overcrowding, but as a
> means of adding 30 days of education. When it came time

for me to begin to make headway with this initiative, I really intended to just make an administrative decision. I would just pick the schools and do it. Democracy got in the way. Someone stood up in a public meeting and said the board ought to survey and get the public's opinion about year-round education. And the board thought that would be the democratic way to do it. And surveys, as they typically do—especially when they are reported in the newspaper—drew all the negative people out. And we were sandbagged through the newspaper and a coalition to do away with year-round schools to the point where I lost the project completely. The board then in their frustration—this defeat also hurt the image of the school board—turned to me with a kind of "how could you do this to us" attitude. The board is happy to be written up in *Education Week* when initiatives such as this spark positive comments—but they really don't like it when there are complaints.

When asked to describe factors that influenced a recent major decision, another superintendent provided a response suggesting an effort to move away from a bureaucratic-like structure.

One decision I made here was to eliminate regional superintendents from our central office staff. And the reason was a perception—which tends to be more political in one sense but a reality in another—that this structure was a bottleneck in the district. Things would get to the regional superintendent's office, like an assistant superintendent's office, and it would stop there. And there was a sense of bureaucracy and power-building that just stopped things from happening—and that the superintendent's vision was not being implemented out in the field. So I abolished all those positions and created comparable positions which I call lead principals. I'm trying to get people to understand that I'm moving to a decentralized system. This requires me to increase the authority and responsibility of my building-level administrators.

A third superintendent emphasized the tensions between seeking input and maintaining responsibility for key decisions.

I think superintendents do have choices in making decisions. The way I operate is that I really try to get advice from a number of different people. And I try to sift through that advice quickly because I don't think you can sit on it. I'm not a person who is going to sit on a decision. I'll make the decision—either right or wrong—and then assume responsibility. We really do involve parents, teachers, and everybody else in the decision of who gets to be principal. And although this is still my decision, I, for the most part, take the recommendations of the people, because that is part of the process. There's been three or four times when I've refused their recommendation or reversed their order—taking their second recommendation over their first—you know, because of race, gender, or just my personal feeling about the process. And when that happens, people get mad.

This superintendent went on to say that cooperative decisions are more complex than they appear on the surface. For example, school-based management is designed to provide the community and teachers with a greater voice in school governance. And although this goal is democratically defensible and related to other positive outcomes, such as staff morale and parental support, it nevertheless raises a number of red flags for those responsible for school district administration.

Survival and Decision Making

The superintendents were very conscious of the fact that the average tenure for someone in their position was less than 3 years. This consideration was often mentioned in discussions about decision making. Several in the Reference Group expressed the opinion that not much could be accomplished if the top executive changed every few years. One noted,

My hope is that we can get people into these jobs who can survive long enough to actually make some difference. But I think that's going to be very difficult. I now understand clearly why people only stay in these jobs 2 years, or 2½ years, or whatever the average is. And unless a number of things change, I think that situation is going to continue. And the rapid turnover makes things worse. Because you have this constant change in top leadership, and the superintendents don't control the school districts. All of this instability impacts negatively on the districts.

Later, this superintendent was asked how long it would take to make a difference in an urban school district. He replied,

It would take you 10 years. I mean, I know that's absurd, but I can tell you, you can't do it in 3. I think you're just scratching the surface in trying. . . . It's taken me 2 years to really hone in on a lot of stuff. And even now, you leave meetings where you think you've resolved problems and they keep cropping up elsewhere. I've talked to other superintendents who tell me they don't think you can make these impacts in 2, 3 years. That it takes much longer. I talked to Superintendent Ingwerson, who was the [national] superintendent of the year last year. Hell, he had been in Louisville for like 10 years. He told me it took him 8 years to get to the point where he was at. So, I think it takes awhile.

When asked how long one needs to remain in a position in order to make a significant difference, another superintendent felt that new appointees should make a minimum of a 5- to 10-year commitment. He went on to say,

Stay there long enough to get some things done. . . . I tell my Board I plan to retire from this school district because I'm going to stay here to see these programs through. . . . But I think that is a weakness in our urban superintendents. They should make their commitment up front. And make decisions based on children—you can't go wrong when you do it that way. I think we go wrong when we start making decisions based on adults.

Would superintendents approach decisions differently if they had more job security? That is difficult to answer because security is only

one of many considerations. Even when large-district superintendents enjoyed relatively long tenures, many chose to use rationality
and politics as their primary guides. It is logical to assume, however,
that some superintendents would devote greater attention to objectives that take longer to implement and are more difficult to assess.

Democratic Decision Making and Responsibility

What happens if a school council violates the law in making employment decisions? Can the superintendent ensure equal educational opportunities in the district if schools are making their own
decisions about curriculum, instructional techniques, textbooks, technology, or budgets? Today, tensions between democracy and managerial responsibility, between democracy and efficiency, may be greater
than at any other time in history. These concerns were discernible in
the superintendents' comments as they alluded to the myriad of ethical or legal issues that grew out of school reform initiatives.

Discussing the dilemma of democratic leadership, Blumberg (1985)
drew distinctions between academic answers to decision making and
those that must be supplied by practitioners. He observed that a
superintendent's world of work is neither abstract nor academic. It
is mired in political realities—realities such as trying to decentralize
governance in a school system in which a majority of board members
may feel that teachers already have too much power, or realities of
having to listen to many viewpoints and demands about a controversial program such as outcome-based education.

Corwin and Borman (1988) alluded to another situation that often
spawns conflict for those who attempt to govern democratically:

> District administrators are held accountable for things they
> cannot always control. This condition is a product of decen-
> tralization processes within formally centralized school dis-
> tricts. School districts are organized officially as hierarchies.
> Implementing educational policy is legally and politically
> the responsibility of high-level district administrators. How-
> ever, in practice only certain decisions are centralized. Many

others have been decentralized, and administrators can never fully control such responsibilities. (p. 212)

There is a tremendous strain between the need to control and democratic beliefs, and it continuously surfaces as school board members and influential citizens express differing philosophies.

Because urban superintendents clearly do not live and work in a perfectly rational and fair world, it is both myopic and unfair to assume that many of them are cautious about sharing power simply because they are bureaucrats. Their concerns relative to decentralization usually go well beyond inflexible management dispositions predicated on the acceptance of bureaucratic theory. They often entail recognition of political, economic, ethical, professional, and legal realities that superintendents encounter on a daily basis. Superintendents often worry about whether ideas such as choice and site-based management will indirectly lead to inequity or greater levels of racial and economic segregation. They worry that parent councils may set standards that are either too high or too low. Unfortunately, the public does not always understand the complexities of these issues, and when the superintendent is less than enthusiastic about implementing new ideas, he or she is often accused of protecting personal power.

Final Thoughts About Decision Making

Judgments about decision making are extremely difficult because each instance of administrator behavior is an intricate mix of complex variables. But in general, comments from superintendents in the Reference Group support the belief that most decisions are made in a political frame. Superintendents expressed an awareness that their tenure would be determined not by long-term educational improvements, but rather by their ability to manage conflict and resources.

Although many comments made to me might have been self-serving, I found that these administrators uniformly accepted responsibility for making difficult decisions. In almost every interview, major initiatives were identified as personal projects. In many respects, demands for school reform have made the urban superintendency an even higher risk job, especially for those practitioners who are unable to move away from long-standing practices that have proven to be successful in the past.

As work environments become more turbulent, there is less and less predictability to the problems that superintendents face (Leithwood, Steinbach, & Raun, 1993). Access to information, via technology, also is changing the conditions under which administrators make decisions. In essence, today's superintendents are playing in a different game. The ballpark may be same, but the rules of the game have changed. Under these circumstances, adaptation becomes more critical than ever before.

SEVEN

PROBLEMS SEEN BY SUPERINTENDENTS

*America's children are truly an "endangered species." And
educators alone cannot "fix" the problems of education.*
                                        —Harold Hodgkinson

Current community contexts in which public education is delivered across America are significantly different than they were in past
eras. Public schools are, of course, direct reflections of the ecosystems
in which they function. Consider several contemporary situations
that exemplify the transformations that have occurred:

- As a whole, our society continues to become increasingly multicultural. In several states, such as California, Florida, and
  Texas, many communities now have "minority-majorities."
- An ever greater proportion of children and adolescents live in
  poverty.
- The two-parent family that includes a working father and home-
  making mother has become the exception rather than the norm.
  Two-parent families, including those in which both parents are
  employed full time, make up only about one third of current
  families (Kirst & McLaughlin, 1990).
- Youth-against-youth violence is reaching epidemic proportions
  in virtually all parts of the country.

Such changes are pervasive, but they have been especially pronounced in big cities. Critics claim that urban districts are impersonal, are far too large, and provide unsupportive learning environments (e.g., Maeroff, 1988). Demographic statistics certainly support their claims.

- Although 38% of public school students belong to minority groups, up to 90% of the students in some urban districts are minority (Tanner, 1989).
- Although 20% of all children grow up in poverty, the percentage is over 70% in many urban school districts.
- About 45% of males enrolled in urban secondary schools were shot at or threatened by a gun on the way to or from school during the past few years (Portner, 1994).

In addition, the urban school context is characterized by public perceptions of decreasing academic standards and performance, increased student problems of all sorts, eroding tax bases, and growing resistance to tax increases from business and large property owners.

Far too often, the public has looked at the quality of urban education and the performance of urban superintendents as if all public schools were on equal footing. With this myopic perspective, critics have tended to concentrate on selected academic tasks and to encourage comparisons of average student outcomes. Perhaps the best example involves comparing the norm-referenced test scores of students as a means of judging whether schools and school districts are successful. In grading our public education systems, would-be reformers have tended to pay little or no attention to the socioeconomic status of students. They pretend that issues such as poverty, crime, deplorable family conditions, and child abuse have no effect on students. Accordingly, they conclude that children in wealthy suburbs do better than children in inner cities simply because they and their teachers work harder.

We ought to remember that the work of school administrators is context specific. Decisions, successes, and failures are heavily influenced by the sociocultural and political environments in which the programs are delivered. Accordingly, functional descriptions of work behavior need to be predicated on a three-dimensional framework that integrates the person, the task, and the conditions under which individual administrators must address specific tasks. For precisely this reason, we must fix in our minds the social, economic, political, and cultural conditions of urban life and the bureaucratic-like nature of urban school districts when we consider problems as they are articulated by urban superintendents.

Perceptions of Problems

As pointed out in the previous chapter, urban superintendents rely heavily on their personal beliefs when making decisions. No doubt these beliefs are affected by their perceptions of their communities and their organizations. That is to say, beliefs and perceptions are related.

Commonalities

In both the written survey and interviews, superintendents in the Reference Group identified problems in their work and the severity of those problems. The survey contained 24 issues commonly identified by the media and found in the professional literature, and the respondents were asked to rank the severity of each. A Likert scale from 1 (*not at all serious*) to 5 (*extremely serious*) was used as a rating scale. Results are shown in Table 7.1, which also includes comparison data from Ornstein's (1991) relatively recent study of large-district superintendents (the two surveys contained some identical items).

It is noteworthy that the two problems superintendents identified as most severe are related to economics: lack of financial resources for their school districts, and the poverty of the families whose children attend their schools. The next three most serious problems relate to social and community conditions.

The concern for money is universal in urban education. In this and the previous chapter, we see that the superintendents cite a lack of financial resources as their greatest problem and financial considerations as the primary factor in decision making. This outcome needs to be considered in light of the fact that per-pupil expenditures among urban schools vary widely (see data in Resource C). Although some

TABLE 7.1 Superintendents' Perceptions of Problems Confronting
Their School Districts

Problem	Reference Group Mean[a]	Ornstein (1991) Rank
Lack of adequate financial support	4.5	1
Poverty	4.4	
Deterioration of family	4.1	
Lack of public understanding about education	4.1	
Crime in the city	3.9	
Parental support	3.8	7
Condition of school facilities	3.7	8
Image of urban life	3.7	
Overcrowding in schools	3.5	2
Gang violence	3.5	
Crime/vandalism at school	3.4	
Employee unionism	3.4	
Student use of illegal drugs	3.3	3
Racism	3.3	
School board interference	3.3	
Teacher competency	3.2	5
Child abuse	3.2	
Administrator competency	3.1	
Inadequately prepared professionals	2.8	
Student alcohol consumption	2.8	3
Interference from elected officials (e.g., mayor)	2.7	
Loyalty, support from staff	2.5	
Employee theft	2.3	

a. Scale is from 1 to 5; 1 = *not at all serious*, 5 = *extremely serious*.

districts, such as Rochester, New York, have extremely high per-pupil expenditures when compared to other districts, others are quite low. Former Baltimore superintendent Richard Hunter pointed out that during his tenure in that district, the city's public schools were faced with "a myriad of problems" but still had "the lowest expenditure per pupil among the largest school systems in the state" (Hunter, 1990, p. 11).

Interestingly, most of the problems that were highly ranked by superintendents in the Reference Group are external to school districts: That is, they are largely beyond the school district's control. Some are reflective of general societal conditions that frequently are more pronounced in urban areas, such as poverty, 4.1; family deterioration, 4.1; crime, 3.9; and gang violence, 3.5. Others are directly related to school funding, such as inadequate financial support, 4.5; condition of school facilities, 3.7; and school overcrowding, 3.5. Conversely, factors that could be considered more internal to school operations were among the lower ranked items (e.g., employee theft, 2.3; staff loyalty, 2.5; inadequately prepared professionals, 2.8; administrator competency, 3.1; and teacher competency, 3.2). Factors that have been traditionally perceived to be especially troublesome to superintendents occupied the midrange of ranked items (e.g., employee unionism, 3.4; school board interference, 3.3).

Interview comments supported the pervasiveness of inadequate financial support as a significant problem. For example, one superintendent stated, "If I were to prioritize the problems of urban schools, funding would have to be at the top of the list." Superintendents volunteered a number of reasons for the financial crisis during the interviews. One felt the lack of resources was exacerbated by "the antitax sentiment that is moving across the country" and "the large percentage of households . . . who don't have school-age kids."

Another superintendent reiterated that the absence of school-age children is a problem, terming it "the shrinking political constituency of public schools." He stated, "When you look at who attends school versus who pays and who votes, the lessons we learn from our referendum keep hitting me in the face." This superintendent's district had recently had a referendum soundly defeated. Demographics indicated that parents of the district's students, the majority of whom were poor and did not own property, had supported the referendum. Meanwhile, property owners, many of whom were elderly, childless, or had grown children, were overwhelmingly against the referendum. Although normally a significant percentage of this latter group did not vote, they had voted in unprecedented numbers during the referendum election.

A third superintendent pointed out how state-mandated reforms negatively affect financial conditions in urban districts:

People, that is legislators, have a tendency to refuse to address the needs of urban school districts. . . . The majority of

the school districts in our state are much smaller [than ours],
. . . so decisions are being made mainly for the smaller school
districts.

One superintendent also discussed the relationship between pressure group demands and resource needs. He noted that pressure groups
were not "sensitive to the increased resources needed to meet the
demands" they requested of school districts. In part, many who seek
more services believe that schools already have too many resources
that are not used efficiently.

Joseph Fernandez provided an example, from his tenure in Dade
County, Florida (where he served as superintendent prior to becoming chancellor of the New York City schools), of how pressure for
additional programs translates into increased financial resource needs:

In Miami we had to put together a program on gun awareness for elementary school kids. There had been a series of
tragic accidents. . . . There had also been the unaccidental kill-
ings, altogether enough to make us see the need in a gun-ob-
sessed society for some strong indoctrination on the ultimate
peril of firearms. What does "put together a program" mean?
It means that people have to be trained. It means developing
curriculum (nobody writes one for nothing). It means doing
research on it, then evaluating it, then implementing it.
(Fernandez & Underwood, 1993, p. 3)

Relatedly, superintendents noted the effect that social phenom-
ena had on school finances. One superintendent spoke about the financial costs for schools associated with addressing violence:

Clearly, the larger issues at stake are community impacts on
school systems—like getting all the money that we spend on
school safety. You get all the cartoons and all that and people
can say whatever they want, but in the world we live in with
the level of violence, I'm not going to sit here and not take
precautions to try to make our schools safer. I mean, you
have to do it. . . . I mean, you can do preventive stuff, and we
do nonviolent intervention, and all that stuff in the curricu-

lum, and we try to teach kids different ways of resolving problems other than through violence, but if their whole environment reflects violence, then you've got to counter it.

According to a 1994 report published by the Council of Great City Schools, violence and gang-related activity was identified as the number one issue facing urban schools. Nearly 83% of the member school districts identified it as a crucial problem; however, only 18% of all school districts nationally concurred (Ottinger & Root, 1994).

Superintendents also saw financial resources as being linked directly to student achievement and meeting public demands. One superintendent observed,

Research says that for poor African American kids lower class sizes in the lower grade levels are especially important. But unless you can get additional classroom space you can't lower class size. And then there are the people who want us to get off of bussing. Well you can't get off a bus if there's no school in your neighborhood. So we have these large attendance areas in black communities because of the way we went about doing desegregation. So all I'm saying is that you can't have it both ways. You can't say, we're not going to build buildings, but we want you to stop bussing. We want you to do a better job of educating kids but we're not going to give you any additional resources to do it.

The dire financial straits of urban school districts also pervaded other sections of the interviews. In response to a question regarding changes in the urban superintendency, one administrator replied,

I don't think the urban superintendency has changed that much. The magnitude of the problems has probably grown. ... What has changed is that urban citizens are finding themselves in a financial crisis more than ever before to deal with those issues. And there's less money coming from the federal government for programs to support those issues, and so if there is a difference it's less resources to deal with issues that were always out there.

Another superintendent cited the effects of a recent financial problem his district had faced.

> We had gone through the last 2, 3 years without any salary increases—last year we had to cut $30 million out of the budget. We eliminated 457 positions, put about 300 people on involuntary leave of absence. A horrible financial condition. . . . That was a horrible issue that consumed so much of my time. Trying to deal with cutting the budget, dealing with employee unrest as a result of involuntary leaves and transfers of staff. Dealing with all kinds of frustrations among staff if they had jobs but were transferred. It was a problem that impacted us all year long.

The depth of financial cuts is an issue that was also mentioned in one of the interviews.

> We've been in a downsizing mode for the last 7 or 8 years, and that downsizing has occurred primarily at the central office level—at a time when demands and expectations are increasing. . . . We've attempted to do what we are able to do to maintain resources at the building level, but because of the number of years that we've been at this, the cuts are affecting kids and they're also affecting the schools themselves.

References to family poverty were not quite as prevalent, although frequent references were made to various aspects of the milieu of urban problems. One superintendent noted,

> Conditions have become increasingly more complex because of the whole issue of diversity, equity, and the condition of the students relative to wanting to learn in schools, wanting to learn or being motivated to learn because of the home environment and the influences of society in general.

Another superintendent expressed it this way:

> I think that right now the cities in America are literally tinderboxes. . . . We see increasing numbers of children for whom

every day is literally a fight for survival, and parents who don't know what the children are doing, who are in an almost hopeless state of controlling or taking care of their children. The alienation that exists toward society in general, that is something that schools will have difficulty overcoming regardless of the organizational models or the instructional models. And that is a frightening situation . . . [the] sense of hopelessness among parents and among so many young people—hopelessness that leads to alienation and vindictive action against other individuals.

The interviews also produced signs of bewilderment related to the public schools' being unfairly blamed for the social and economic problems of big cities.

The blame that is placed on schools for the street violence that is occurring within our city and across the country—that's very frustrating to me because it's not really the schools. . . . Coupled with that, the lack of progress in general made not only locally, but statewide and nationally in getting beyond the attitude of just merely tolerating diversity. . . . I don't see a whole lot of real attitude and behavioral changes. A lot of rhetoric, but I don't believe society and people in general have made much progress in getting beyond the mere tolerance-of-diversity attitude.

This superintendent later elaborated on this point by illustrating a course of action he was taking and by proposing a direction for society. He illustrated the interactive efforts he and the district were making to curb youth violence:

Our role has to be that of a major player working with the city, working with law enforcement agencies, working with parents, working with churches, working with the community in general. . . . I, with several staff, meet with the chief of police and his senior staff monthly to check signals, and to converse about how we are working together, where the problem spots are, what we can do to assist each other. In addition to that, I meet with the leadership of the various segments of the community to try to stimulate an attitude on the part of the community leadership that it is a community problem, not just a school problem.

As the interview was concluding, this superintendent asked to share one more thought that linked commitment to diversity and financial commitment.

Can I say one other thing? . . . Until society . . . makes a commitment with their dollars rather than just the rhetoric and gets beyond this whole business of merely just barely tolerating diversity to a commitment to do everything we can to help the young, especially those who are socially disadvantaged, I do not see a lot of hope for the city schools in the future.

Differences

Given the fact that urban schools vary substantially in areas such as total enrollment, geographic size, and financial resources, it was not surprising to find some contextually specific differences in the problems that confronted members of the Reference Group. One of them related to the amount of time the superintendent had been in office. Often those who are newly appointed are encouraged (or mandated) to change the governance structure of the organization. More to the point, they are employed with hopes that they will alleviate pressures being placed on school board members relative to school reform. But the task is daunting, because many key officials in the school system support the existing culture.

One superintendent who had only recently assumed his position alluded to this problem when he talked about trying to move the school district toward decentralization.

As I see it, my biggest challenge is creating a central office staff that clearly understands the nature of a decentralized school system and the services that need to be provided. What I'm trying to do is create a mechanism that says central office is no longer going to be that overseer of that person that's out there. . . . Central office is going to be more like the clinical-assistance-type operation where schools will be able to broker their services and tell us what they need. . . . Trying to get our central office to change its focus is of real concern.

Although many contextual variables contribute to superintendent perceptions of problems, it is surprising that so few superintendents in the Reference Group identified reform, restructuring, or organizational change as one of the three greatest needs facing urban districts. The several who did were relatively new appointees. School reform and restructuring was, however, ranked fourth in the top 10 current issues identified by superintendents in the entire Council of Great City Schools in 1994. Just under 60% of the superintendents saw it as a major issue, compared to 20% of all superintendents in all types of districts (Ottinger & Root, 1994).

Dramatic change in student enrollments, either rapid growth or decline, is one of those more pressing matters that affected perceptions. This is best exemplified by the comments of a superintendent who indicated that his district had grown by "11,000 students last year, and about 10,000 the year before." The growth rate included "350 non-English-speaking, foreign-born students per month." In this particular district, growth had "overshadowed" all other problems and was responsible for change being placed on the back burner. The superintendent of this district noted,

We're having to find so much money for construction that we have gone to technology as a stabilizer between some of the things we might have done and trying to accommodate language problems. Not only are we getting that 350 students per month in our kindergarten through 12 programs, but all their parents are going to school also. Our adult programs are now overwhelming us with all those parents wanting to be trained in both language and skills to be able to work in this country.

The influx of immigrants had caused many of this city's "established" residents to move to the western suburbs, areas still located in the county-wide school district. The superintendent noted,

As they move to the west, they want new schools out there. And there is this belief that if they get these new schools in the "white west," the inner-city schools need to be rebuilt. So almost all you're going to get out of me today is the frustration of the job that relates to growth and financing.

Compare these comments with those of a superintendent who had just made decisions to terminate a large number of employees because of declining enrollments and budget reductions:

I mean everybody is talking about downsizing now . . . and you're cutting this and cutting that at a time when those millions of dollars in lost resources should be enhancing programs for students who come to us.

Although most superintendents alluded to management problems that are only indirectly related to the teaching and learning process (e.g., finances, growth), several specifically mentioned teaching, learning, and student achievement as key concerns. For example, one superintendent stated,

Right now, the whole achievement issue is still the big issue with urban education across the country as well as right here. We're not as bad off as some urban districts, we've made great progress. But I still see where we need to improve the whole teaching/learning process. And it's more of a retraining aspect to train our personnel to teach the population we serve. And I often tell staff it's not their fault. . . . They were trained in higher education based on the way they teach, and the way they're being trained is not what is needed. . . . We want to raise our standards, and people must understand that raising your standards and not changing the way you teach or the way you educate youngsters will not get the job done.

Another superintendent cited his biggest problem as overcoming the obstacles that stood in the way of student achievement:

[The biggest problem is] to turn around a school district that continues to fail a significant number of kids. And how do you remove all the excuses and whatever it is that we use— it's not just excuses, it's also the kind of impediments that exist. In terms of content, how do we develop education in kids? [How do we deal with] the things that happen to kids before they ever get to us? But in the end, the kids simply have to achieve in spite of whatever else is going on. That, to me, is the major problem I confronted.

Is Professional Preparation a Problem?

Through much of the 1980s, a number of reformers and critics suggested that the preparation of school administrators needed to be improved. These included leading groups (e.g., National Policy Board for Educational Administration, 1989) and individuals (e.g., Hallinger & Murphy, 1993) within the specialization of educational administration. Suggestions, however, were usually generic, calling for a broadening of the curriculum, higher admission standards, and greater rigor in classroom work and internships for administrative preparation programs.

But is the preparation of educators to become urban school superintendents seen as a special problem? A number of individuals close to the position think that the answer is "yes." As a result, several preparation projects have been created since the late 1980s to serve the needs of those already in practice (e.g., Superintendents Prepared, a program that enrolls approximately 30 practitioners who aspire to become big-city superintendents) and those pursuing formal graduate study (e.g., a new doctoral program for aspiring urban superintendents at Harvard's Graduate School of Education). It is far too early to tell whether these efforts will have a significant impact on either increasing average tenures or permitting meaningful changes in existing school cultures.

We know relatively little about the application of that portion of professional knowledge that is gained in graduate study. There is a sense that practitioners' skills are learned largely on the job, and because

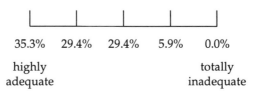

35.3%   29.4%   29.4%   5.9%   0.0%

highly   totally
adequate   inadequate

FIGURE 7.1 Perceptions of Academic Preparation Among Reference Group Superintendents

the tenures are declining, individuals may have less and less opportunity to hone their skills in successively difficult positions (Crowson, 1987). If this is true, staff development efforts that stress craft knowledge are essential to professional practice.

There are many defensible arguments for greater rigor in the professional preparation of all school administrators. There are also many points to be made for focused study and experiences for those who intend to work in urban settings. These contentions should not lead to expectations, however, that professional preparation alone will change what is occurring in big-city school districts, because there simply is no empirical evidence to substantiate the claim that practitioners fail in their jobs because of inadequate academic preparation.

Members in the Reference Group were asked specifically whether their academic studies adequately prepared them for their jobs. They responded by assigning a rating on a 5-point scale ranging from *totally adequate* to *totally inadequate*. Only one superintendent in the group thought that his academic preparation was somewhat inadequate. The results are illustrated in Figure 7.1.

Specialized academic study for the urban superintendency and staff development efforts may encourage competent individuals to pursue these positions, and it may provide them with political survival skills. But given the inescapable mix of community context, organizational culture, specific problems, and administrator, we should be cautious about overstating the effects of this single criterion. In addition, we need to consider the fact that there is little agreement on what knowledge and skills are of most worth to urban school superintendents. Superintendents who succeed in one district may fail in another. Without a uniform, national curriculum for professional preparation, improved programming for urban administration is apt to move in many different directions.

Regarding the need to provide specialized professional preparation for urban administrators, two factors need to be considered. First, professional education ought not be considered as simply a 3- or 4-year graduate school experience; it needs to be lifelong. Employers should commit to providing employees, even superintendents, with structured learning opportunities. A number of larger districts—for example, Cleveland—have developed internal academies to serve this purpose (Crisci & Tutela, 1990). Second, no matter how well prepared superintendents may be for the challenges they face, their prospects for making a difference are small if current problems of urban life and the political conditions of urban education remain intact. Members in the Reference Group indicated that their effectiveness was attenuated by a multitude of problems deeply rooted in their communities and organizations, not by incomplete or misdirected professional preparation.

Additional Thoughts on Problems

Discussions with superintendents in this study revealed that two financially related concerns were pervasive: (a) a lack of financial resources for urban school districts, and (b) the poverty of the families whose children attended their schools. A variety of opinions were voiced regarding the causes of these problems, ranging from antitax sentiments to middle-class flight to uncontrolled immigration of poor families to urban districts. The common feature of these suggested causes is that they are factors almost always beyond the control of both school boards and superintendents. Other recent studies of big-district superintendents also produced findings indicating that the lack of fiscal resources is foremost in their minds when they discuss problems (e.g., Ornstein, 1991).

As anticipated, the superintendents continuously intertwined social conditions with the problems they faced in their organizations. Crime, illegal drugs, and violence exemplified community-based concerns that recurred through the interviews. One administrator even suggested that America's big cities had once again become tinder-boxes—a condition that obviously existed when cities like Detroit and Los Angeles experienced riots during the 1960s. Disruptions in Los Angeles in 1993 certainly provide us with one piece of evidence that he may be correct.

Although there was clearly a great deal of frustration in their comments, the superintendents also expressed a significant amount of hope. I sensed that each cared deeply about being able to create educational environments that could somehow counterbalance the appalling conditions in which many of these children were forced to live. In the context of discussing problems, it became increasingly apparent to me that society, or more specifically, the officials who speak for society, and urban school superintendents were pulling in different directions. While elected officials and leaders of corporate America keep demanding internal reform in public education, the school chiefs keep looking outward for financial assistance and newly created social programs. In discussions of primary problems in their work lives, superintendents made little mention of pressures to reform schools. With regard to reform, efforts of school administrators and so-cietal leaders appear uncoordinated, and at times even contradictory.

In many ways, suggestions to improve the role of urban super-intendent are plagued by the same myopic perceptions that prevented meaningful school reform during the 1980s. That is, critics keep con-centrating on the symptoms while ignoring the underlying causes of the crisis. In the case of the superintendency, this has included such simplistic diagnoses as judging that inadequate academic prepara-tion is a primary reason why urban school executives fail. This sort of conclusion, analogous to blaming lazy students and inept teachers for public education's shortcomings in 1983, simply lacks empirical evidence. Such assessments only serve to redirect attention from far more cogent issues, such as poverty, crime, and deterioration of the traditional family.

EIGHT

WORK LIVES OF URBAN SUPERINTENDENTS

One of the most surprising observations about the superintendency is the relative lack of inquiry into how these executives manage the internal organizational affairs of their school districts.

—Robert Crowson

In his 1985 book on the school superintendency, Blumberg noted the conflictual nature of this administrative position. He wrote, "One cannot understand what the superintendency is all about unless one also knows that the undercurrents that move the position and the person in it are almost always conflictual in nature" (p. 2). Although the reference was in respect to school superintendents in general, data collected from the Reference Group indicate that the statement remains relevant when applied specifically to those who work in urban settings.

The Work of Superintendents

Few studies have attempted to describe the actual work lives of school superintendents, quite possibly because both personal and situational variables found in the work are multifaceted and difficult to control. Available information, nevertheless, tends to confirm that

89

although the jobs are hectic and contain a variety of tasks, many practitioners are able to adapt by constructing coping mechanisms (e.g., Friesen & Duignan, 1980). Studying executive behavior in the late 1970s, Morris (1979), for example, found that compared to top executives in other types of organizations, superintendents often relied on internal organizational support. That is, they had contact networks that were oriented toward interactions with subordinates, but this was done at the cost of reduced external contacts.

Observations of practice indicate that time and information burdens often serve to deter or discourage administrators from engaging in detailed daily planning (Duignan, 1980). From the earliest days of urban school districts, the daily activities of the typical superintendent have been described as frenzied. In a late 1960s book, Burbank (1969) described a superintendent's time commitments as follows: "The hours flow into days, and the days into weeks and months, in an endless round of official duties, small and large. No hour of the day can be counted free of work" (p. 91).

There is an old adage that "there are only so many hours in the day." Those who understand school administration usually agree that all superintendents maintain rigorous schedules requiring long hours at work. Does time allocation, however, adequately explain the difficulties of a position? Probably not, because superintendents do not face the same set of problems across school districts. Some are immersed in financial difficulties, others find that most of their work is directed at managing declining enrollments, and still others are preoccupied with mediating labor disputes.

Attempts to understand superintendents' work have often entailed collecting data on superintendents' perceptions of it. These perceptions are the product of a multitude of influences. For instance, Burlingame (1988), reviewing a study by Khleif in the late 1970s, explained how they can be shaped by experiences in graduate study. Candidates for superintendent certification had often been "resocialized" by their graduate school experiences (after an initial socialization that occurred when they entered practice as educators). Aspiring administrators were often encouraged by professors and peer students to change their self-perceptions and behavior so that they ceased to see themselves as teachers and started to identify with managerial roles. Although many would argue that conditions in professional preparation have changed markedly since the early 1970s, many of the sitting urban superintendents completed graduate school in that era.

Experience, personal needs and wants, motivations, personality, and a host of other variables also contribute to perceptions of the superintendent role, and ultimately to conceptualizations and actual behavior. Central to such perceptions, however, is the relationship between superintendent and school board. Superintendents often discuss their work in a political context that focuses largely on interactions with board members. Even though it is well established that these relationships are not uniform—that is, some superintendents dominate their boards and others are submissive—practitioners often see their work in this context because they know that board members are primarily responsible for both their job security and their power. Unfortunately, our understanding of board-superintendent relationships is made more difficult by the fact that practitioners possess multiple motives for establishing and maintaining both submissive and dominant relationships. A review of literature and research by Burlingame (1988), for example, exhibited how a considerable number of superintendents dominated their school boards as a method of preventing interference from community groups and individuals.

Self-perceptions are also affected by ideal roles, especially those that appear in professional literature. It is in this context that superintendents are prone to talk about themselves as instructional leaders and to relate to teachers as their professional peers. In fact, it is not uncommon to hear the comment, "Ideally, I would like to be the instructional leader of the school system, but reality dictates that I manage and put out fires." Thus when superintendents talk about their work, especially when participating in research, they tend to move between their actual role (which is largely political and managerial) and their ideal role (which is largely professional).

Job Changes and Comparisons with Small-District Superintendencies

Interviews conducted with Reference Group members indicated that tensions among the managerial, political, and professional roles of superintendents continue to exist. For the most part, group members expressed the belief that their jobs had not been altered markedly by reform efforts during the past two decades. One commented that "the job is essentially the same as in the past, the problems have just been magnified."

None said that their managerial and political roles had been weakened by attempts to restructure schools. More precisely, they did not indicate any mounting expectations for them to devote more of their efforts to being instructional leaders. They uniformly expressed the belief that their jobs entailed more management and political activity than in past decades, and they perceived these requirements to be more demanding in urban districts than in other demographic settings.

When asked how their positions compared to superintendencies in other types of districts, members of the Reference Group thought the problems they faced were substantially (94%) or somewhat (6%) more difficult. The most probable reasons cited for this condition were social and economic woes in big cities, the larger size of urban districts, and a more intense political environment. The view that the superintendency was unique in urban settings was evident in the comments of one of the superintendents:

> I will spend two, three, four times as much time dealing with security [as suburban superintendents]. Dealing with security and discipline—that's number one. Secondly, I will deal two or three times as much in trying to resolve budgetary problems and finding financial resources. I will have to spend a great deal more time—two to three or four times more time— in working with instructional improvement to try to begin bringing students closer to national norms. In most suburban school districts the kids perform pretty well regardless of what the superintendent does. The issue of parent dissatisfaction with schools—I will have to spend more time with that than most suburban superintendents will spend. Because of all the problems that come to bear in the cities . . . the extreme poverty conditions, the violence, the resources—all those frustrations come together, and parents aren't satisfied, and they think that the schools can resolve all those problems. The business community, in their frustration with the schools, have a tendency to say, "Well, if the schools would just do

their job, why, things would be ok." They just don't want to address the issues of unemployment and poverty and neglect and abuse and . . . all those forces that happen in large cities.

Another said that the size of the organization was a factor that set urban superintendencies apart:

The magnitude of the problems probably has grown, and that probably depends on the size of district you are in.

And a third superintendent pointed to community turmoil as a relevant factor:

The major impact in my judgment on the urban superintendent in the last few years has been that urban school districts have more turmoil. They usually have more financial problems [than other types of districts].

Comparisons With Previous Jobs

Reference Group members often compared their work to previous jobs that they had held. This appeared to be true regardless of whether they had acquired their positions via internal promotion or whether they had been hired from outside the school system. In all instances, they characterized their urban superintendency as much more difficult than their previous jobs.

One superintendent who had served as deputy in the same district for 3 years prior to moving up to the top position summarized his thoughts after receiving the ultimate promotion:

When you are in a system and spend 3 years as the deputy superintendent running the day-to-day operations of the school system . . . moving up to the top position, I thought I knew how to be a superintendent. But you must experience sitting in the seat before you can understand the role of the superintendent. So my first 60 to 90 days were very rocky because there were several issues I had to address. One was superintendent-board relationships. I had to develop that. I was following a superintendent who believed in wining and dining his board to get information and get things accomplished. I call that the whole political process. I . . . believed that you work hard and you do the job and you concentrate on children and you're out there advocating for children—but that's not true. So I had to take a step back after about the first 60 to 90 days and reevaluate this whole process, because I was fighting battles within the organization. I was able to make the adjustment, and right now the superintendent-board relationship going into my third year is one of the best, based on what I hear other superintendents complaining about.

Previous experience seemed to have no influence on the way the superintendents described their jobs. They uniformly saw their jobs as highly difficult. But those who had held a variety of positions prior to entering the urban superintendency provided more detailed responses. This was clear in the following comment:

I don't think there is any job that I've had that remotely compares with this one in terms of the level of difficulty, the level of stress, and the overall pressure that you have to deal with on a day-to-day basis. And I think you know that I've held some fairly . . . you know . . . responsible and difficult positions. I mean, in the governor's cabinet and the Department of Health and Human Services. But none compares to this. It is just—this is difficult to describe—what the job is really like. So I would say that there just is no comparison to the other jobs.

Another superintendent alluded to the behaviors he thought were absolutely essential in his job.

I think that one of the most critical elements for being successful in a large organization . . . is the ability to do many things and switch from many things. But I think the successful people are individuals who, in the process of doing all those things, are able to see how those issues relate to some major goals or major priorities for the school system and for the job. Yeah, you do have to manage. You do have to try to pull political forces and political groups together into alignment, and you do have to deal with the intellectual issues of the teaching/learning process. But there has to be some kind of unique way where you see what you are doing, how it all works together, and that it's all coming together toward a directed purpose. One of the things that I have noted is that if the district is in a period of just almost utter turmoil, it is extremely difficult to keep any sense of vision or sense of general purpose about you. All of your energies and focus of attention seem to revolve around just getting from one crisis to another.

Characterizations of Work

As mentioned in earlier chapters, input from the Reference Group provides a portrait of practice that indicates that work is (a) extremely demanding and (b) more frequently and directly political than pedagogical. What follows in the remainder of this chapter are glimpses of how superintendents perceive their work and their daily activities, information that is intended to encourage further exploration of the topic and to enrich our meager understanding of how these leaders actually spend their time.

Reference Group superintendents were asked about their job-related responsibilities and the amount of time allocated to them. One set of questions required them to respond to a series of semantic differential inquiries regarding their feelings about their work lives (see Table 8.1). The semantic differential pairs were adapted from the work of Holmes (1991)—work he completed as part of a study of the chief executive officers (CEOs) of Canadian school districts.

Among the six characteristics for which differences between the Reference Group and the Canadian superintendents were noted, one stood out because the difference was so great. Whereas the superintendents in the Holmes study characterized their work as "high predictable," the urban superintendents characterized their work as "high

TABLE 8.1 Comparison of Reference Group Work Life Responses
and Holmes's (1991) Results

Characteristic	Reference Group	Holmes (1991)
Hectic-serene	very high hectic	very high hectic
Exciting-calm	very high exciting	very high exciting
Predictable-surprising	high surprising	high predictable
Demanding-easy	very high demanding	very high demanding
Political-pedagogical	very high political	very high political
Technical-humanistic	neutral	high humanistic
Professional-administrative	high professional	high professional
Collegial-independent	high collegial	high collegial
Authoritative-subordinate	high authoritative	high authoritative
Isolated-interactive	high interactive	neutral
Leading-following	very high leading	very high leading
Frustrating-fulfilling	neutral	high fulfilling
Well rewarded-poorly rewarded	high well-rewarded	very high well-rewarded
Satisfying-stressful	neutral	high satisfying
Proactive-reactive	high proactive	high proactive
Calculated-spontaneous	high calculated	high calculated
Democratic-bureaucratic	high democratic	(not asked)
High status-low status	very high high status	(not asked)

surprising." A number of scholars have suggested that organizational turbulence almost always reduces predictability, and conditions within the urban districts may partially account for the outcomes. The lack of perceived predictability of urban superintendents' work is especially cogent in light of the fact that bureaucratic structures are predicated on rational behavior.

Differences with respect to isolation-interaction may be explained by two conditions. First, big-city superintendents are often forced to spend a great deal of their time with officials from outside of their organizations (e.g., mayors, city council members). Urban superintendents usually get appointed to a number of boards of directors, committees, and the like. Second, the size of urban districts often results in layers of administration, so that the superintendent must spend a great deal of time with deputies, associates, and assistants.

Thus the "high interactive" rating from Reference Group members may be due to conditions that necessitate higher levels of contacts with persons external to the school system and with staff administrators.

Most dominantly, superintendents in the Reference Group characterized their work lives as being *hectic, demanding,* and *exciting* rather than *serene, easy,* and *calm.* As one superintendent said during an interview, "There's just not one moment of free time, and you are absolutely on a hundred-yard dash throughout the day."

Superintendents in the Reference Group also strongly characterized their positions in survey responses as *high status* and *political* and viewed themselves more as *leaders* than as *followers.* This also came out in interview responses. For example, when asked if he wore the three different hats of statesman/politician, scholar/educator, and manager/supervisor, one superintendent replied:

Two out of three isn't bad—I don't know about the scholar. Probably with all the years here and knowing the community, I probably have served well as a politician because I have been able to bring the business community into guarding the political decisions some of the people have made. The manager—I probably spend as much time with something big managing as I do about creative or scholarly ideas. I don't put myself into the scholar category—more in the manager.

Another superintendent affirmed the political nature of the position but had a broader view on other aspects.

You're always engaged in some political thing out there. But to me, that is the nature of the job. That's what I think this job is. These jobs are so difficult, they require a lot of different skills in order to, first off, survive personally, but also to try to move any kind of agenda forward. You've got to know politics. You've got to be able to deal in public relations. You clearly have to know something about education and something about organizational behavior. You obviously have to have some verbal skills and analytical skills—and then you put the whole political thing on top of that. It's a daunting task!

Prominent in survey responses, but slightly less prominent than previously cited characteristics, were characterizations by the superintendents of their positions as more *interactive* and *collegial* than *isolated* and *independent*. Descending still further in rank order, they felt the positions were *well rewarded* and *professional* and that work life was *surprising* rather than *predictable*. Commenting on the unpredictable nature of his work, one superintendent noted:

> You don't ever know as a superintendent what emergency is going to pop up that you have to deal with. Something happens at a school, and you have to go even though you have a schedule. Or you never know when . . . the city council will come calling saying, "We want you over here." Or my board will call and say, "We need a meeting to sit down and talk with you." Unless they can show me . . . that this is something that's really critical to attend over what I have scheduled . . . I just refuse to get away from my schedule as much as I possibly can. There are days when I don't have a choice. . . . If a fire occurs in one of the schools . . . I have to go. Or if a shooting occurs at a school, I have to go.

There were some apparent contradictions in the ratings. For instance, although Reference Group superintendents saw their roles as *authoritative* rather than *subordinate*, they simultaneously viewed themselves as *democratic* rather than *bureaucratic*. In addition, they characterized their work as *calculated* rather than *spontaneous*, but at the same time *proactive* rather than *reactive*. Finally, they viewed their positions as *professional* rather than *administrative*.

Reference Group superintendents were neutral (i.e., scores fell in the midrange between the two characteristics) regarding whether their work was more *technical* or more *humanistic*, more *frustrating* or more *fulfilling*, and more *satisfying* or more *stressful*. However, this does not mean that the characteristics represented by the two sides of the semantic pair are not strong aspects of the work lives of superintendents in the Reference Group. It is more likely that both sides of the pair are strongly present.

Although the responses from the Reference Group were similar to those obtained by Holmes (1991) in his study of all superintendents in Ontario, Canada (response rate = 64.7%), there were some dimensions on which the two groups differed:

- Reference Group superintendents characterized their work as highly *surprising*, whereas Holmes's (1991) Canadian school CEOs characterized it as highly *predictable.*
- Canadian CEOs characterized their work as highly *humanistic*, whereas Reference Group superintendents were neutral on whether it was more *technical* or more *humanistic.*
- Reference Group superintendents characterized their work as highly *interactive*, whereas Canadian CEOs were neutral on whether it was more *isolated* or more *interactive.*
- Canadian CEOs characterized their work as highly *fulfilling*, whereas Reference Group superintendents were neutral on whether it was more *frustrating* or more *fulfilling.*
- Canadian superintendents felt they were more highly *rewarded* than Reference Group superintendents.
- Canadian CEOs characterized their work as highly *satisfying*, whereas Reference Group superintendents were neutral on whether it was more *stressful* or more *satisfying.*

Time, Activities, and Location of Work

Over the years, studies of principals and superintendents have revealed a rather high level of dedication to work. A recent survey sponsored by the *Executive Educator* magazine, for example, indicated that long work weeks were common in school administration. But despite job-related stress and recurring complaints about salaries, most of the 900 practitioners surveyed were content with their jobs (Boothe, Bradley, & Flick, 1994).

As might be expected, Reference Group superintendents also indicated that their work extended well beyond the standard 40 hours per week. When asked to identify the average number of hours devoted to work per week, their responses ranged from a low of 50 hours per week to a high of 112 hours. The average work week was a mean of 73 hours and a mode of 70 hours.

TABLE 8.2 Reported Use of Vacation by Reference Group
Superintendents

Use of Vacation	Number of Vacation Days
High	25.5
Low	0
Mean	12
Median	10 (2 weeks)
Mode	15 (3 weeks)

How do they find relief from such a demanding schedule? Most said they look forward to vacations. In this regard, one superintendent spoke of the need to protect personal time.

For instance, last week for my vacation [my wife and I had planned] to go to Cape Cod, and it was cleared [on my calendar]. "Well, we're going to Cape Cod and I don't care what comes up." I made that clear to people.

But interestingly, the total vacation time used by these administrators was only 2 to 3 weeks per year—a level that is probably much lower than found among comparable CEOs in the private sector. At the extremes among the group were a superintendent who took no vacation days in the previous year and another who took 25 days (see Table 8.2).

Superintendents who participated in interviews were asked to outline a typical workday. In many instances, they elected to describe the previous day's activities because those events were still fresh in their minds. Although examining a single day's work certainly does not provide a comprehensive picture of how urban superintendents spend their time, the information serves to exhibit the hectic nature of their roles.

Described workdays began as early as 5:15 a.m. and extended as long as 11:00 p.m. at night. The latest any of the superintendents said they began their workday was 8:00 a.m., with none completing the workday before 9:00 p.m. The most dominant activity was meetings; the average number per day was identified as 6.6.

One superintendent commented on the difficulty he faced in limiting the number of meetings he attended:

> Today I started out with a meeting at 7:30 a.m.—a breakfast to talk about the Boy Scouts. At one level, you know, why am I talking about the Boy Scouts? Well, it's because of who asked me. You're constantly balancing your time in trying to decide who you meet with because everybody says they have to see you. But because I'm from here and grew up here and I know so many people, it's an added burden—because of my history in the city. More people can get to me because they know me and because they know where I live. So I start off with a meeting talking about the Boy Scouts using our building. I mean, I shouldn't have been there, but, you know, I did it.

Typical participants in meetings that superintendents attended were described as "anyone and everyone." Specifically cited in descriptions were teachers, principals, district office administrators and staff, business people, food service personnel, associate superintendents, school board attorneys, community service agency personnel, teac   , College Board personnel, univers   ers, city managers, youth agency pers   ⌐   d presidents, and charter school pers   many superintendents had daily inte   se contacts generally involved gov   rs, and the like. Certainly nota-ble   nts made any reference to meet-ings

One of the superintendents who was interviewed for this book had kept a log of the previous day's activities. During his interview, he used those notes to relate his activities:

> Yesterday from 5:00 to 5:15 in the morning I drank a cup of coffee and read the morning paper—in my office. From 5:15 to 5:45, I went through my mail and did the daily paperwork.

From 5:45 to 6:45, I prepared a speech that I needed to make
at a breakfast meeting. From 7:15 to 9:00 I attended the breakfast meeting and presented my remarks. From 9:00 to 9:30 I
drove across town to attend a board meeting at the chamber
[of commerce]. From 9:45 to 10:30 I attended that meeting.
From 10:30 to 10:40 I drove to my office. From 10:45 to 12:00
I met with the middle school and high school principals' group.
From 12:00 to 1:45 I met with various staff, made about a
dozen calls to disgruntled patrons on the budget, on tax increases and the cut. One forty-five to 2:00, I drove to the
teachers' association office. Two o'clock to 4:15, I met with
the board of directors of the teachers' association, and that
was not a very pleasant experience—but that's what I did.
From 4:15 to 4:30, [I] had a postmortem of that session with
two of my staff who were with me. Four thirty to 6:00, [I]
went back to finish my paperwork for the day, responded to
a number of telephone calls and staff requests. Six fifteen, I
left the office to drive home. From 6:30 to 7:30, I had a drink
and had dinner with my wife. From 7:30 to 8:30, I began to
prepare my remarks for my administrators' and supervisors'
meeting tomorrow because this is the beginning of the school
year and of course there's a major message that needs to be
delivered. From 8:30 to 9:30, I responded to several calls, read
the paper, and watched part of the news. And at 10:15 I died!

When asked how this day compared with other workdays, the superintendent replied, "It's very typical."

Reference Group superintendents were asked how many evenings per week they spent in work-related activities. Thirty-one percent said three nights per week; an equal number (31%) said four
nights per week; and 25% said five nights per week. Only 13% responded that they worked two nights per week, and none indicated
that they worked as few as zero or one night per week or as many as
six or seven nights. The average number of evenings worked by Reference Group superintendents was 3.7. Almost all the superintendents
who were interviewed referred to frequent weekend work activities.
These included such things as banquets, out-of-town meetings, school-
based functions (e.g., plays, musicals), and picnics.

Involvement in community affairs has been considered a high priority for urban school chiefs. Data obtained from the Reference Group certainly reinforced this belief. All the superintendents indicated at least a moderate level of activity in community affairs, with 67% indicating a high level of activity in community affairs. One superintendent described his involvement in the community as follows:

> I serve on about 27 nonpaying boards. And I don't get involved with a board if I can't attend the meetings and be there to have input. In that area I might have stretched myself, but I felt it was necessary because I was trying to bring this community together and change the community's perception of me as superintendent. . . . On Saturdays I'm always speaking some place or at some function dealing with education. . . . And on Sundays, there's not a Sunday that I don't get an invitation to speak in one of the churches. . . . I attend my church on the first Sunday, and on other Sundays I'm visiting other churches, usually in the capacity of speaking at the 11:00 a.m. service. . . . Then I tape a TV show every week which we play in the schools—it's about 5 or 10 minutes, and is based on whatever issues are in the community.

The primary location in which the Reference Group superintendents' work occurred was in their offices (see Table 8.3). On average, 35% of superintendents' work occurred in their offices, with another 21% of the activities taking place elsewhere in the school district's central office complex. Thus over half of the work hours of the urban superintendents in the Reference Group were spent in one building—the central administrative offices. The remaining work hours were split fairly evenly between time spent in the community (average = 19%), in schools (average = 15%), and in other locations (average = 9%).

Work location data, however, indicate that those in Reference Group did not adhere to prescribed patterns of behavior. For example, time spent in one's own office varied from 75% to 20%. Time spent in schools also exhibited a considerable range, from 5% to 35%. These dissimilar patterns of time allocations and locus of work activities were also apparent in comments made during the interviews. For example, one superintendent in describing his workday observed,

TABLE 8.3 Characterizations of Urban Superintendent Work:
Location

Location	Factor	Figure Reported
Superintendent's office		
	Highest	75%
	Lowest	20%
	Average	48%
Central office building (outside superintendent's office)		
	Highest	40%
	Lowest	2%
	Average	20%
Schools		
	Highest	25%
	Lowest	0%
	Average	12%
In the community		
	Highest	35%
	Lowest	5%
	Average	19%
Meetings outside the school district		
	Highest	35%
	Lowest	0%
	Average	6%
Other		
	Highest	35%
	Lowest	0%
	Average	5%

> And if I am lucky, somewhere in there I will get to go to a
> school even just to visit, and this will probably be just 1 day
> out of the week. . . . If I am lucky that will take an hour or
> maybe 2 hours out of a week.

By contrast, another superintendent included school visitation as a
part of his regular weekly agenda. He noted,

> On Fridays I do not have any appointments. On Fridays I
> visit schools. I get up in the morning and pick a school and

start visiting. I try to visit six or seven schools on Friday. Now also I have breakfast with my teachers in their various buildings. If they are willing to come in 1 hour early, I will sponsor breakfast and we just have a roundtable discussion with teachers. Last year I think I made 153 visits into schools, being with teachers and students.

Also showing considerable variation was the time these superintendents spent outside the boundaries of their districts. Some indicated that they rarely leave the district. These superintendents tended not to be highly involved in national groups, nor did they see attendance at regional or national meetings as a very high priority. Yet some of the superintendents noted that as much as one third of all of their work time is devoted to regional and national functions (e.g., professional associations, commissions, boards of directors).

Final Thoughts on the Work Lives of Urban Superintendents

Data from the Reference Group suggest that urban superintendency is uniformly demanding with regard to time. That is to say, all respondents had long workdays, devoted three to four evenings a week to their jobs, and almost inevitably spent some time on weekends in work-related activities. Yet where they spent that time and the areas in which they chose to involve themselves exhibited significant variation.

In part, differences in how superintendents spend their time are probably attributable to a combination of personal and situational variables. The degree to which a superintendent is able to set his or her own agenda for time allocation often depends on both pressing issues and the philosophy of the practitioner. Although some complained that they never had time to visit schools, at least one devoted a full day per week to this activity.

Of special note are two outcomes regarding perceptions of work. Urban superintendents saw themselves as having levels of interaction, suggesting that their ability to work with others is critically important. In addition, they characterized their work as highly unpredictable. This finding provides another reason in a long list of reasons for dismantling the bureaucratic structure of urban districts.

NINE

REWARDS AND FRUSTRATIONS

Effective superintendents will be those who manage the seemingly contradictory elements of the job: to develop leadership both from the top down and from the bottom up, to be both tough and gentle, to be both leader and follower.
—Jerome T. Murphy

Speculation regarding the reasons leading educators to accept and subsequently leave the urban superintendency still abounds. Many continue to surmise that money and power are the primary attractants, and that politics and inadequate resources are the prevalent causes for exits. More complete data on such matters would provide us with a richer understanding of the rewards and frustrations of the position.

At least two considerations deter fuller understandings of what practitioners see as the positives and negatives of their work. First, urban superintendents constitute a heterogeneous group whose motivations are probably inconstant. Accurately assessing their feelings is a difficult task. Second, questions about job satisfaction are often answered in a "professionally correct" manner. That is, practitioners respond to questions by referencing their ideal roles. This tendency has been especially evident in the contrasting opinions given by those who strive to remain in the job and those who know they are exiting or have recently exited.

Potential Rewards and Common Frustrations

Some observers would argue that former Washington, D.C., school superintendent Hugh Scott was prophetic when he made the following comment in a 1976 article that appeared in the *Phi Delta Kappan:* "The feel of impending doom is pandemic. If the record of the past seven years continues, most big-city superintendents will not remain in their positions long enough to accomplish anything. The turnover and turmoil raise serious questions about the viability of the position itself" (Scott, 1976, p. 347). Scott's judgment was predicated on several conditions that remain as valid today as they were when he first articulated them. For example, he noted that major cities exemplified the negative consequences of social disorganization and deterioration; he pointed out that urban school districts woefully lacked the resources needed to meet their responsibilities; and he warned that because urban superintendents had to respond directly to diverse groups and individuals, they had to become consummate politicians in order to survive.

In that same issue of the *Kappan,* however, the retiring superintendent of Buffalo, New York, Joseph Manch (1976), contended that Scott had painted an overly pessimistic picture of the urban superintendency. Although he was in agreement with Scott's views about community-based problems, he felt that able educators could still do well in the job. Manch, however, was not typical for individuals holding this executive position. He had just completed an 18-year tenure as superintendent of schools in Buffalo.

These two perspectives, although written many years ago, still delineate the contrasting views held by prominent educators—including members of the Reference Group. Many who have recently exited from the urban superintendency, especially those who had relatively short tenures, argue that Scott was correct. But there are others who still harbor the dream of taking the helm of one of the nation's largest school systems and being able to survive for a relatively long term.

In part, individuals see the potentialities of the urban superintendency through their personal frame of reference. Some are by nature optimistic. Whereas one individual may assess 3 years of dedicated work as a major professional accomplishment, others may judge tenures of less than a decade to constitute failure. In much the same way, conclusions about rewards and frustrations are often in the eye of the beholder. Regardless of its difficulty, the urban superintendency remains a high-visibility position. And even many of those who leave unwillingly after just a few years are often able to acquire other positions that are equally or more lucrative and prestigious.

In his national study of school superintendents, Glass (1992) found that superintendents in large school systems (defined as those with 25,000 or more students) when compared to superintendents in lesser enrollment districts were the most likely to find self-fulfillment in their job. In this group (N = 145), 21% indicated that their level of self-fulfillment was moderate, 77% said it was considerable, and only 2% said it was little. Although some of the superintendents in this category may not have been employed by big-city districts (some may have been from large suburban districts), the finding shows that those in the largest districts are the most likely to find self-fulfillment in the superintendency. In that same study, Glass found that two issues were especially likely to drive a superintendent from a large district: lack of community support, and financial matters. Two additional studies recently found money and politics to be the primary frustrations faced by big-district superintendents (McCurdy & Hymes, 1992; Ornstein, 1991).

A study of women in urban superintendencies, conducted by Wesson and Grady (1994), found that the ability to make a difference in the lives of students was the most satisfying element of the position. The authors' research provided insights into the professional orientation of the practitioners they studied.

Rewards and Frustrations:
Perspectives From the Reference Group

What specifically do superintendents find satisfying about their jobs? Superintendents in the Reference Group were asked to identify the three facets of their jobs that were most rewarding. Unquestionably, the most frequent response focused on being able to make a difference in student outcomes. This was expressed in many ways: "helping provide a quality learning environment," "helping instruc-

tional staff to do their best," "seeing improvements in student outputs," "creating opportunities to improve academic achievement,"
and "assisting colleagues to educate students."

The second most rewarding experience related indirectly to the
power of the position. Examples included the following dimensions
of the job: "the authority to be a change agent," "being able to set
goals," "opportunities to lead," "opportunity to make the organization more productive," and "being in a prestigious position." The
third highest reward revolved around community interaction: "gain-
ing community support," "chance to improve public perceptions,"
"being an advocate for children in the community," and "engaging
in community activities." Interestingly, none of the superintendents
listed those extrinsic rewards that tend to receive the greatest attention from the media (e.g., salary, fringe benefits), and only one superintendent noted school board support among his or her three choices.

Interestingly, superintendents often pointed specifically to an accomplishment that was readily apparent to the community when
identifying rewarding elements of their jobs. One superintendent described his most satisfying accomplishment as follows:

> I enjoy the job or I wouldn't stay with it. I personally enjoy
> the challenges—that's just my nature—I guess that's one of
> the reasons why I'm in it. My close friends have asked, "Why
> on earth did you take that job, and why are you staying with
> it?" I just enjoy the challenge! I also feel very strongly that
> children in large urban areas are those with the greatest needs.
> These children need help, and there are a lot of people who
> are not willing to work with them. So I have a very strong
> personal commitment there. I have a sense of satisfaction
> from being able to bring some progress to this school district.
> We're in a major renovation program. We're renovating over
> 100 schools and building three new schools. We were able to
> pass a $131 million dollar bond issue, and that was in addi-
> tion to the money the courts ordered the state to pay for
> improvements. Seeing this come together has been extremely
> rewarding.

A similar response was provided by another superintendent:

I guess the most satisfying experience was passing a $10.4 million tax levy at a time when finances were tight. This community rallied around the school district, and we were able to pass the bond issue by about six or seven thousand votes. And this was really gratifying because the system needed the money to carry out our plans.

One superintendent identified relationships with students and staff as particularly satisfying:

For me, the most satisfying experience is the relationships I establish with kids. I try to work hard on that. It helps that I'm on TV a lot, because the kids know me. They stop me, you know, because of where I live; and they stop by and talk to me. That kind of relationship is good. The other thing is the permanent relationships I have established with the very fine people who work in the public schools. We really have some superb people in this system.

By contrast, another superintendent laughed when I asked him to identify his most satisfying moment and then provided this brief answer:

The most satisfying was about 2 weeks ago when I gave notice that I was going to retire!

The superintendents also shared their three greatest job-related frustrations. Among the many identified, two clearly stood out as recurring themes: a lack of fiscal resources, and the pervasive nature of politics. These responses are quite congruent with findings from other recent studies.

Among the other frustrations mentioned by Reference Group members were the following:

- An unrealistic workload
- The "inability to move as quickly as we should"
- Apathy on the part of students and staff
- School board members managing instead of setting policy

* Battling elitism and racism

Elaborating on their greatest frustrations, the superintendents often described dilemmas that involved conflicting interests among the school district, employees (or their unions), and students (or their parents). This condition was exemplified in one superintendent's description of how he tried to close several schools. His recommendation was preceded by an internal study that indicated that fewer but more comprehensive schools would benefit students. He presented the school-closing plan to the school board, assuming that those who constituted the school-community would be reasonably objective in reacting to his recommendations. As he said, "I thought every one would agree to put the students' interests first." But instead, he encountered stern resistance as parents, students, and staff adopted the slogan, "Don't close my school."

Another example of tension created by the conflicting interests of the organization, employees, and students was provided by a superintendent who described a teachers' strike in his district:

> The most disappointing experience for me was a teacher strike that lasted 11 days. And it was very painful—a mental strain on me. We kept our schools open all 11 days. And from my standpoint, I could not understand the purpose of the strike. There were certain issues we felt we should address, and they were based on the needs of the organization and needs of clients—the young people. And some people did not understand this aspect of it. I felt that in the 7 years I have been in the system, we had developed collaboration, a team-building concept with our union. But unfortunately, the new union president did not believe in the collaborative philosophy. So the whole strike was frustrating. They wanted an adversarial situation—so it became a battle. Attacks on me were a constant. They did not concentrate on issues, they concentrated on the superintendent.

Several superintendents in the Reference Group described more general conditions in their jobs when they talked about their frustrations. The following exemplify these assessments:

In my own style of operation, I thought I could solve everything. And I'm not going to be able to do that. It's frustrating
to know you are going to leave something undone for the
next superintendent.

I think the most frustrating thing is just trying to get something done, trying to change the way that the system oper-
ates. You've just got so many barriers. I usually talk about
the fact that when you really look at it, everybody is organized to protect themselves. And in my view, this system is
really adult driven, and that's the biggest frustration. Then
it's just all of the crap, you know, day in and day out. You're
in a no-win situation most days because every time you make
a decision you tick somebody off. And that's just the way it
is. It took me a long time to accept that and be able to deal
with it.

There are so many of those [frustrating experiences] that it
would take a week for me to answer.

But regardless of whether superintendents discussed specific situations or the general nature of their jobs, they almost always mentioned the frustrations caused by politics, declining social conditions,
and inadequate funding. These issues were simply pervasive. Reflecting on his tenure in New York City, Joseph Fernandez commented
that all urban schools, and New York City in particular, had funding
problems. He also indicated that the political nature of contemporary
school boards was not readily understood by the public. Many citizens, according to him, view school boards much as they do university boards of trustees or corporate boards of directors, a perception
he found to be in error:

The difference, quite simply, is night and day. Boards of trustees
oversee, but you never hear them telling college presidents
how to run the history department. Trustees and corporate
boards don't meet as often, don't get involved in the nitty-gritty,
and are far less likely to be swayed by politics. (Fernandez &
Underwood, 1993, pp. 249-250)

Although urban superintendents were rather consistent in pin-pointing money, social conditions, and politics as major barriers to achieving their goals, they were less than uniform in assessing the implications of these conditions. Some saw the obstacles as basically insurmountable; they had become cynical about the prospect of any-body's succeeding in such difficult conditions. Others were actually optimistic, or attempted to appear so, stating that energetic leaders always find ways to get things done—even under the most adverse conditions.

The Personal Nature of Rewards and Frustrations

Interestingly, the greatest rewards identified by the members of the Reference Group related to the professional responsibilities of superintendents. In part, this may again reflect the tension many superintendents feel between the moral conviction that they are pro-fessionals and the reality that they must function as politicians. There is some evidence that being detached from what is going on in class-rooms tends to make superintendents feel uneasy (e.g., Willower, 1979-1980).

Rewards most frequently cited by members of the Reference Group are accomplishments that are most directly associated with the facili-tating role of administration (e.g., helping instructional staff, creating opportunities, assisting colleagues). By contrast, there was virtually no discussion of extrinsic rewards—especially those that relate to personal benefits, such as salary, fringe benefits, and opportunities for other jobs. Even so, it is hard to imagine that remuneration, visi-bility, recognition, and expanded opportunities upon leaving the ur-ban superintendency do not serve as motivators for some of these practitioners.

Collectively, statements about frustrations revolve around a single circumstance. Although the superintendents recognize how inade-quate funding, social ills, and rampant politics deter their organiza-tions from moving in desired directions, they realize that there may be little that they can do to eradicate the conditions. Their frustrations are exacerbated by the probability that they have very little time to make a difference. It seems inevitable that urban superintendents are constantly being pulled in two directions, one leading them to rely on political compromises, and the other encouraging them to enact the ideal role of professional.

At the start of this chapter, the views of two urban superinten-dents who were leaving their positions in the mid-1970s were sum-marized. Even though the two men were in agreement about the severity of community-based problems endemic to big cities, they held substantially different views about the potentialities for success in the urban superintendency. Interestingly, comments from the Ref-erence Group members showed the same agreements and divisions. What is unclear is whether these positions are explained by person-ality factors such as being an optimist or pessimist. There have been numerous studies probing a relationship between life satisfaction and job satisfaction, but results have failed to prove a causal relation-ship (Judge & Watanabe, 1993). Most probably, perceptions regarding the potential to succeed are once more an intricate mix of personal and professional experiences.

TEN

CAREER

Effects on Personal Life and Commitment to the Job

The life of the administrator may be viewed by others as reactive, segmented, and replete with critical decisions, but there appears to be an almost Darwinian natural selection process. Among those who persist there is, usually, a positive perception about the role.

—Michael M. Milstein

Any job as visible as the urban superintendency naturally generates questions about life outside of work. Living in a fishbowl, school executives must make many decisions that affect the way they live and their relationships with those closest to them. But how does the need to make adaptations affect one's well-being? Do the long hours take a toll on family life? Although there have been efforts to analyze influences that exist outside of the school district, these studies have almost always concentrated on relationships in the community rather than family and personal life.

Another personal dimension that is explored in this chapter involves commitment to the job. At what point in life do these educators decide that they want to be urban superintendents? And once they reach this position, what is their level of commitment to the work?

Effects on Personal Life

Jim O'Connell, executive director of the 741-member New York State Council of School Superintendents, was quoted by Goldstein (1992) as saying, "Stress is becoming a greater liability of the job than ever before. I've never seen it tougher" (pp. 9-10). Although such observations are rather common for both superintendents and principals, they are disputed by some researchers who have found that administrative jobs are only mildly stressful (e.g., Wiggins, 1988). Milstein (1992) directly questioned whether the case of "administrator burnout" has been exaggerated. Examining the work lives of superintendents, he cited poorly designed research studies and generalizations as ample cause to question whether a majority of these practitioners really find their jobs unduly stressful.

Responses obtained from the Reference Group show that perceived levels of stress are dissimilar. Because all urban superintendencies are demanding and immersed in discord, this outcome suggests that stress may be more a matter of individual disposition than job. Some administrators are able to cope with constant conflict and associated pressures, whereas others find these conditions damaging and intolerable. There are even some individuals who appear to thrive on conflict.

Consider the following sentiments expressed by one of the superintendents regarding stress in his job:

I don't think there is any job that I've had that remotely compares with this one in terms of the level of difficulty, the level of stress, and the overall pressure that you have to deal with on a day-to-day basis. And . . . I've held some fairly . . . responsible and difficult positions . . . but none compares to this. It is just—this is difficult to describe—what this job is really like. . . . There just is no comparison to the other jobs. Now there are similar skills [required] in the sense that you have to deal with boards and you have to deal with committees. . . . There's dealing with the press. There's people skills. . . . There are common skills that are transferable, at least from the positions I have had, but I just think that the level of stress, the pressure, and the number of issues that come at you almost minute by minute—there's just no comparison. One of my staff members described working here as like "being under siege," and I think that that's how you feel a lot of days. Just because of what you have to deal with. And I think it's all taken place within the context of a society that is just antigovernment, anti-institution, for a lot of good reasons. Then you've got the particular issues of public schools and people's view about public school. You bring all that together and it's a very difficult situation.

One great concern about top executive jobs is personal health. When asked whether the urban superintendency had adversely affected either their physical or their mental health, only 18% said that it had to an extensive degree. The issue of personal health is too frequently ignored by both school boards and candidates.

Influence on one's personal or family life was found to be more pronounced. Concerns such as marital relationships, spending time with children, and a lack of privacy were frequently voiced by Reference Group members. Nearly 80% admitted that their jobs had affected their personal lives extensively.

Several of the superintendents commented about the ways in which their jobs affected marital relationships and family life.

I think my wife has found it [the job] more frustrating than I. I think because I have been in this system since 1957—when I started as a teacher and moved up through the ranks—I was always on the move and always involved publicly. So I didn't have to adjust to a new community when I became superintendent. It was more frustrating for my wife, because I spent much more time away from home than I had on any other job. The adjustment was only hers. The children are grown and out in the community. It might have affected their families having Grandpa's name in the paper and people knowing who I was in relation to my children. But it didn't affect me much.

I'm divorced, and my divorce became final shortly after I accepted this job. That was my second marriage. If I were

married, I don't know how I'd get my work done. Because
by the time I drag home, I have little energy left.

Because of the hours demanded by this job, I try to take my
wife with me whenever I can to meetings or banquets. If it
had not been for a very supportive and understanding wife,
I would have been out of this job long ago. My children are
grown, but I still try very hard not miss any of their activities.
But there is the reality that the job is most of your life if you
do it the way it needs to be done.

There were a number of comments that indicated that these superintendents gave a great deal of thought to how their work made
them adjust their personal lives. Interestingly, one superintendent
cautioned that worrying too much about stress may cause total de-
tachment from work—a condition he saw as more serious than the
stress itself.

You've got to somehow build up your defense mechanisms
without becoming so objective that you become detached.
Because I still think you have to feel some of this stuff. At the
moment you no longer feel it or you just become detached
from it, I think that's definitely a very dangerous place to be,
in my opinion.

Developing the metaphor of school district as theater, Deal, Lison,
and Deck (1993) noted that superintendents find that they are always
on stage. How a superintendent plays this role depends on several
factors, "including one's understanding of the script, interaction with
an audience, and awareness of personal style and values" (p. 28). All
urban superintendents are constantly in the public eye, but their reactions to this condition take many forms.

The comments I received from members of the Reference Group
regarding the consequences of their work to their personal lives certainly fortified the notion that individual personalities and philosophies
were more important than the job. Although some of the superintendents lamented the fact that their private lives were nonexistent and
although a few said the job had taken an extensive toll on their per-

sonal health or personal life, there were those who liked being in the limelight.

Career Selection

One of my curiosities focused on the point at which these individuals decided to become urban school superintendents. Did they actually plan to end up in this job, or did serendipitous turns in life just put them there? Among teachers, for example, it is not uncommon to find that career choice was made rather early in life. Because there are growing indications that fewer educators are aspiring to become superintendents (Daresh & Playko, 1992), issues related to career intentions are becoming a greater concern.

Answers provided by the Reference Group suggested that most urban superintendents do not target this position as a career goal when they first enter the profession. About one in three developed the objective to become an urban superintendent in mid-career, and slightly over half said they never had this aspiration. Only three of them set the goal to become an urban school superintendent as early as the first few years of teaching. These findings are basically congruent with outcomes of research published by the American Association of School Administrators in the early 1990s, which indicated that typically individuals decide to seek the superintendency while serving as a principal (Glass, 1992)—a condition suggesting that it occurs most commonly in mid-career.

Unexpectedly, all 17 members of the Reference Group said they had no regrets about choosing education as a profession. Given a chance to retrace their steps in life, each professed a commitment to again be an educator. And notwithstanding the stress and hectic pace of their present positions, 77% said that they would again attempt to become a school superintendent. Yet when asked if the urban superintendency was a good job, only 23% agreed and only 12% strongly agreed. These results are not too dissimilar from those noted in a 1958 research project involving all superintendents and conducted by the American Association of School Administrators. In that study, only 1% expressed regret about career choices, and only a third said that they had a job previously that they enjoyed more than the superintendency (Knezevich, 1962).

Thus results from the Reference Group reinforce findings from earlier studies that those who occupy the superintendency tend to have a great deal of loyalty to both education (as a profession) and the superintendency (as a specialization). Even though the odds of serving more than 3 years as superintendent in a given urban district are against them, the individuals with whom I talked expressed no regrets about their careers. And even though the urban superintendency may have lost some of its prestige over the past five or six decades, there was a sense of pride among them in having been able to ascend to one of the very highest positions in their profession.

Commitment to the Position

Nearly 40 years ago, Gouldner (1958) developed an insightful treatise about the organizational behavior of managers. On the basis of what he saw as latent social roles, he categorized practitioners broadly into two groups: cosmopolitans and locals. The former included individuals who typically have a low level of loyalty to their organization but a high commitment to their profession. By contrast, the latter group included individuals who had a high level of loyalty to their organizations but a low commitment to the specialized skills associated with the role. This framework captured my thoughts as I spoke to superintendents and read their input on the surveys.

Some superintendents expressed tremendous loyalty to their current systems; not surprisingly, they tended to be individuals who acquired their positions through internal promotions. Three come readily to mind. Two had never worked in another school district, and the third had vowed not to look for another job. He went so far as to criticize his colleagues for always looking forward to their next promotion (a job in an even bigger and/or more prestigious district). Then there were the true cosmopolitans, who seemed to have a more pragmatic view about their jobs and their ability to survive beyond several years. Although they too spoke of dedication and wanting to help young men and women, they were usually more inclined to accept the likelihood that they might not be in the current position for very long. It is hard to imagine that these basic differences in disposition did not affect the way superintendents approached their jobs or their daily behavior.

The fact that the person is central to explaining administrative behavior is certainly not disputed (Boyan, 1988). Yet little is known about the beliefs of superintendents toward their jobs and their reasons for acquiring them in the first place. As a consequence, there is a great deal of conjecture about the motivations of urban superintendents. Krinsky and Rudiger (1991) wrote that many are enticed to the position by the challenge, the perceived sophistication associated with the job, visibility, and relatively high compensation. Information from the Reference Group convinced me that some of them, especially those who acquired their positions via internal promotions, were in the right place at the right time.

During the interviews, I asked superintendents directly, "Why did you want this job?" One of the more interesting answers follows:

> I have to be honest with you. It's a question that I ask myself. The answer that I give myself is that—and it's true—is that I care a lot about the kids. I don't believe a community can survive if you can't figure out a way to educate kids in the public school system. And if I can somehow make a contribution in that way, then I think I will have made a contribution to a city I care a great deal about. For me this job has no interest in and of itself. In other words, to me it's not a big deal. I shouldn't say that. It is a big deal to be a superintendent in the sense that I think that that's a very responsible position in any community. So from that standpoint, it's a big deal. But the position in and of itself doesn't help me. It only has meaning to the extent that you can do something with the position. Since I don't see myself going to any other place to be a superintendent, it's not a career thing for me. So because I approach it in that way, I assume that's why I continue to try to do it.

A second superintendent cited a similar reason when discussing his motivations:

> My close friends have asked me, "Why on earth did you take that job, and why are you staying with it?" I enjoy the challenge! I also feel very strongly that children in large urban

areas are those with the greatest needs. These children need help, and there are a lot of people who are not willing to work with them. So I have a very strong personal commitment there. I have a sense of satisfaction from being able to bring some progress to this school district. . . . Hopefully that will help us as a school system provide opportunities for children.

A third superintendent was more pragmatic when articulating his reasons for continuing in the position:

I signed a contract. I accepted that contract. I'm committed to the school district. It's a first-class school district. We're doing very well despite all the problems. And I feel committed to doing what I can to help this staff do what's right for the kids who attend our schools. Were it not for the commitment and support of staff, I probably would not be in this job for very long. And I think there's the matter of pride. I'm not a quitter. But how much longer I'm not sure.

Generally, the superintendents gave no indication that they wanted to run away from their jobs. Despite the pressure and difficulties, and despite the reality that the odds of their remaining in their jobs for more than 3 or 4 years were against them, they seemed to be finding satisfaction in their jobs. For some, that may be achieved through visibility, compensation, or other extrinsic rewards. But all seemed to realize that they were in a position to make a critical difference in the lives of others.

Concluding Thoughts

The urban superintendency can be an extremely stressful job, but for some it clearly is not. The position can have a deleterious effect on marriages and family life, but for some it has resulted in enhanced spousal relationships. Disparate consequences exhibit rather clearly that individuals adapt to the challenges of the urban superintendencies in unique ways. What remains unclear are the personal characteristics that contribute most to these unique adaptations.

In light of the fact that the number of educators who aspire to become superintendents is declining, there are several career-related questions that deserve the attention of the profession. It is hard to imagine that most physicians or heads of major corporations would say that they did not plan to get where they are. Yet this was the case with many of the urban superintendents. Instability, politics, and unrealistic job expectations not only affect those already in practice but also serve to discourage future generations of potential superintendents. We have much to learn about why individuals choose to become teachers and why some of them ultimately pursue leadership positions.

ELEVEN

THOUGHTS ON SCHOOL REFORM
AND BUSING

The American people as a whole lack a comprehensive under-
standing of the role of education in a free society.
—George S. Counts

Since 1983, the school reform movement has passed through several distinct stages, and as this has occurred, the plight of urban schools
has received more focused attention. The media have linked poor
student performance on standardized tests to a variety of social ills,
such as violence, crime, drug abuse, and teenage pregnancies. The
cumulative effect has been a decreasing level of confidence in large-
city public schools (Stout, 1993)—even to the point that many gov-
ernmental leaders question whether the negative conditions can be
reversed. In many big cities, the media have provided near-continuous
coverage of problems that permeate both communities and public
schools. And over time, this exposure has taken its toll. Like a hydra-
headed monster, poverty, crime, and social disorder have prompted
middle-class families and businesses to flee. Left behind are those
who have no choice in determining where they live or where they send
their children to school.

Urban School Reform: Direction and Failures

School reform has assumed several different meanings. Especially when applied to big-city systems, the concept can be characterized along a continuum that ranges from conservative to radical (Makedon, 1992). A growing number of critics (e.g., Carlson, 1993) have charged that attempts to improve urban schools have focused largely on politically conservative ideas that advance a basic skills curriculum rather than attempting to build programs that center on the real needs of children. In the late 1980s, for example, the Carnegie Foundation for the Advancement of Teaching (1988) concluded that the reform movement launched to upgrade education throughout the United States remained irrelevant for many African American and Hispanic students in urban schools. A formal report on large-city public schools prepared by this distinguished panel included the following passage:

> In almost every big city, dropout rates are high, morale is low, facilities often are old and unattractive, and school leadership is crippled by a web of regulations. There is, in short, a disturbing gap between reform rhetoric and results. The failure to educate adequately urban children is a shortcoming of such magnitude that many people have simply written off city schools as little more than human storehouses to keep young people off the streets. We find it disgraceful that in the most affluent country in the world so many of our children are so poorly served. (p. xi)

If anything, conditions have worsened since these judgments were rendered.

Jonathan Kozol, author of the well-known book *Death at an Early Age* (1967), concluded after visiting a number of inner-city schools that they are more separate and more unequal than they were three decades ago (Kozol, 1992). Deteriorating conditions in large cities contribute to the fact that public schools in these settings do not fare well when compared to surrounding suburban systems. This is especially the case when such comparisons are the product of district averages from norm-referenced tests covering basic skills. But urban districts, themselves, are not totally blameless for a lack of progress.

Although it is true that social and economic problems are ubiquitous, efforts to reconfigure schooling in many of these systems have, at best, been token. So at a time when superintendents and principals ought to be encouraged to take more risks in implementing needed change, their unlevel playing field prompts them to be defensive.

Superintendent Views on Reform

Although there is common agreement among enlightened observers that school reform initiatives since 1983 have been disappointing, there are those who claim partial victory. They argue that the focus on education over the last 15 years has at least raised public consciousness, increased funding for schools, and resulted in marginal educational improvements. Urban school leaders frequently point to recent efforts to implement popular ideas such as in-district choice or site-based management as evidence that their organizations are not standing still. For example, virtually all member school districts in the Council of Great City Schools reported being involved in district-wide reforms in 1994 (Ottinger & Root, 1994). These included "decentralized decision-making structures, recruitment programs for minority teachers, multicultural curriculum, school based self-assessment, and teacher professional development programs" (p. 5). But are urban schools really engaged in meaningful reform? Or are claims of reform activity political reactions to community pressures?

Comments from urban superintendents point to two primary conclusions about school reform and urban public schools. First, the strategies and methods of the 1980s, namely intensification mandates, failed to bring about consequential alterations in the way schools function. Some argue that efforts to date have been ineffectual because they fail to address the organizational inadequacies of schools. Superintendent Walter Amprey of the Baltimore City Public Schools is one who has concluded that simply doing more with what is in place is insufficient. He said, "There is no question in my mind that we're out of time and we're out of tricks. The whole concept of reform has to carry with it an accelerated, determined, powerful effort to change the culture" ("Involving Cities in Our Schools," 1993, p. 1).

Second, real improvement requires a high level of commitment that is most probable if it is based on a philosophical agreement between school and community. Donald Ingwerson, former superintendent of the public schools in Jefferson County (Louisville), Kentucky, observed that believing in what you are doing is essential to school improvement. One valuable lesson he learned about positive change relates to total commitment. In his district, there were schools dedicated to change, those that experimented with change, and those that wanted no part of change. About the first group of schools he commented, "Those schools, those principals, those students, and those parents who deal in *systemic* reform really do improve" ("Involving Cities in Our Schools," 1993, p. 5). Even more noteworthy was his observation that just dabbling with change may be less productive than preserving the status quo. He found that schools that tinkered with change were essentially less productive than those that rejected change ("Involving Cities in Our Schools," 1993).

Survey questions posed to the Reference Group included several reform-related issues. The superintendents were instructed to respond to statements by selecting one of five response choices from a Likert-type scale that ranged from *strongly disagree* to *strongly agree.*

Three of the reform-related statements focused on societal perceptions of urban schools:

- Urban schools are unfairly judged by the public.
- Urban schools are improving.
- Most citizens want urban schools to improve.

As anticipated, most superintendents, 80%, thought that urban districts were being unfairly judged. Their responses regarding actual improvements, however, were almost evenly divided. Just over half, 52%, indicated that they thought urban schools were getting better. With regard to the public wanting urban schools to improve, most were optimistic. Slightly over two out of every three superintendents in the Reference Group expressed the opinion that the public really desired to see these schools become more productive.

With respect to specific reform initiatives, the Reference Group superintendents expressed mixed feelings as to whether decentralization would improve educational programming in their districts.

Just over half of them agreed with the statement. Yet when asked about the most commonly cited concept of decentralization, site-based management, the results were substantially different. Just over 80% expressed agreement with the contention that site-based management is a sound concept. These results suggest that decentralization, even under the common banner of site-based management, can mean many different things. Tallerico (1993), summarizing decentralization projects in several urban districts, noted that "interpretations and applications of the general concept of site-based management vary widely" (p. 235). In some instances, ideas are put in place by using labels, but the organizational culture remains constant. For example, site-based management may be advertised as a major innovation, but there may be no real loosening of budgetary and policy control from top levels of the district. Decentralization, by comparison, usually carries broader connotations, and thus may be more threatening.

Throughout the 20th century, urban schools have exhibited the potency to ward off interventions that threaten the bureaucracy. Describing mandated decentralization in the Chicago public schools, English (1990) wrote, "The centralization/decentralization dichotomy can be carried within the bureaucracy successfully without leading to the development of internal bureaucratic antibodies being injected into the system from which it ultimately perishes. Bureaucracies are too complex to be so fatally stricken with such a simple malady" (p. 17). Imposed programs, regardless of their focus and intent, are usually rendered ineffectual because the organization mobilizes to defend the dominant culture.

School choice has become another popular topic in school reform. Glazer (1993) presented it as the primary hope for dismantling the massive bureaucracies that control urban schools. He believed that school improvement would be a product of smaller schools in which parents and teachers adhered to common philosophies—conditions often found in urban private or parochial schools. But support for school choice, especially options that extended beyond school boundaries or those that extended to public-private choice, was virtually nonexistent among the superintendents in the Reference Group. Although 71% agreed that in-district choice was a sound idea, only 12% rendered the same opinion with regard to allowing students to

TABLE 11.1 Attitudes About School Reform Issues

| | *Attitudes (Percentage of Total Responses)* | | | | |
Factor	*Strongly Agree*	.	.	.	*Strongly Disagree*
Urban schools are unfairly judged by the public.	0	5.9	11.8	58.8	23.5
Most citizens want urban schools to improve.	0	17.6	17.6	41.2	23.5
Urban schools attract good educators.	0	17.6	58.8	23.5	0
Urban schools are improving.	0	11.8	35.3	35.3	17.6
Decentralization will result in improved educational programs.	0	11.8	47.1	35.3	5.9
Site-based management is a sound concept.	0	5.9	11.8	52.9	29.4
Choice within a school district is a sound idea.	5.9	5.9	17.6	41.2	29.4
Choice among public school districts is a sound idea.	23.5	29.4	35.3	11.8	0
Choice programs that allow students to select public or private schools is a sound idea.	76.1	11.8	5.9	5.9	0

choose any public school, and still fewer, 6%, agreed that allowing students to select any school, public or private, was a good idea.

Generally, Reference Group members held different views on reform-related issues. The two statements that produced the greatest level of agreement pertained to unrestricted choice and site-based management. Detailed results for attitudes on reform-related statements are displayed in Table 11.1.

Recruiting and Hiring the Best and Brightest

One of the reform-related statements included in Table 11.1 that deserves focused attention is "Urban schools attract good educators." This was an issue on which superintendents appeared to be quite candid—only about one in four expressed agreement with the statement. Several commented that urban schools simply cannot compete with wealthier and less crime-ridden communities for the best and brightest in the education profession. And there is some evidence to support this judgment. Compared to their peers in other types of school systems, urban teachers often have lower salaries, work under greater bureaucratic constraints, teach more students per day, and lack basic materials (Ascher, 1991).

The task confronting personnel administrators in urban districts often extends beyond hiring outstanding candidates. Because of demographic conditions, the goal is usually modified to recruiting and employing the best and brightest minority candidates. And ideally, the goal is further modified so that it becomes recruiting and employing the best and brightest minority educators who are themselves products of urban schools. Many administrators believe that teachers who were reared in big cities are more likely than others to understand the culture and challenges that surround the job. Under the best of circumstances, achieving this goal has been difficult, and it is especially so today because the pool of minority teachers in America is actually declining. African American teachers once constituted 18% of the nation's teaching force, but by the late 1980s that figure dropped to 6.9% (Haberman, 1989). With respect to talented students who attended urban schools, Haberman (1989) wrote:

> In an urban school system (which is where most blacks and Hispanics attend school), it is unlikely that the most successful students want to subject themselves to the conditions of work in which they have observed their own approximately 50 teachers and countless substitutes. They have seen ineffective teachers functioning as "lifers" and "burnouts." (p. 772)

Hence teachers who are the most marketable to urban schools often seek safe and well-financed work settings, and they are prompted to do so by insights they gained in early-life experiences.

One superintendent in the Reference Group took a different perspective on the ability of urban districts to attract outstanding educators. He pointed an accusing finger at schools of education, indicating that teacher deficiencies were pervasive and the result of inadequate academic preparation.

> I find a lot of teachers are not competent in their content areas. I want to elaborate, because this is a big issue. You bring in elementary teachers who have taken all of the methods courses but maybe only one or two classes in teaching math or science—and then we employ them and find they are not truly knowledgeable in math or science. At least they are unable to transfer adequate skills to students. So the whole content area issue is a weakness in urban education around the country. And it stems from how they are trained.

In general, the urban superintendents were not optimistic about their chances for improving schools by attracting the best and brightest teachers and administrators. Although a couple saw their inability to achieve this goal as stemming from a generic lack of quality candidates, most believed that they simply could not compete with suburban or smaller city districts. Although salary was a commonly cited reason, especially when the competition for top candidates was between an urban district and an affluent suburban district, the superintendents perceived safety, quality work environments (i.e., being able to work in modern school buildings), and access to resources (e.g., staff development, instructional materials, technology) as the primary reasons for their disadvantage.

Views on Busing

Although not necessarily a reform-related issue, school busing remains a cogent topic for urban school chiefs. As a result of court orders during the 1960s and 1970s, many big-city districts reconfigured transportation zones (Tallerico, 1993) or engaged in desegregation plans with surrounding districts. Most continue today. Therefore the issue of busing to achieve racial balance was raised with Reference Group superintendents. They were asked to express their agreement or disagreement with the following statement: "Busing students to achieve desegregation has been successful in most urban school districts." Only one of the 17 agreed with the statement. This outcome was not totally unexpected for at least two reasons. First, many urban districts have been involved in one-way busing programs that have reduced their enrollments and fiscal resources, and busing some students to suburban schools can attenuate strong linkages between schools and neighborhoods. Second, one-way busing programs have done little to improve racial balance in the inner-city school systems. Statistics published by the Council of Great City Schools showed that African American student enrollments declined in member districts by 4.6% between 1980 and 1990; however, during that same period the decline in the number of white students was 24.9% (Casserly, 1992).

Some observers believe that concerns for economic segregation are now as important as those for racial segregation. During the 1980s, Hispanic student population in districts making up the Council of Great City Schools grew by 44.5%, and many of these students come from immigrant families living in poverty. From 1980 to 1990, the number of students living in poverty in the districts making up the Council of Great City Schools rose from 24.7% to 28% (Casserly, 1992).

Final Thoughts on Reform

This chapter has underscored the fact that urban superintendents were as divided on the question of whether urban schools had improved as they were on the question of whether one could succeed in their job. On several issues, though, they showed very similar views. Most opposed choice programs that would allow students to exit their districts; most thought site-based management was a sound idea. Beyond responding to specific statements included in the survey, members of the Reference Group had less to say about school reform than was anticipated. Compared to social, fiscal, and political issues, school restructuring was clearly not on the front burner.

Although the superintendents did not elevate school reform to be one of their major priorities, they certainly were not indifferent about the topic. Rather, they seemed to be expressing feelings that tinkering with programs and decision making without correspondingly addressing those issues that put inner-city children at risk would have little consequence in improving outputs. As discussed in an earlier chapter, problems superintendents classified as most severe tended to be those over which they had very little, if any, control.

TWELVE

THE PRESENT AND THE FUTURE

Challenges Ahead

The key to decentralization of political power in the United States today is local action.

—John Naisbitt

Contemporary practice in the urban superintendency is neither easy to describe nor easy to understand. A multitude of variables can steer behavior at any given time, and they do not appear in routine patterns. Essentially, they can be classified in five broad categories:

- The general environments (communities) surrounding the school districts
- The organizational dynamics of the school districts
- Academic preparation and socialization into a profession
- A myriad of social, political, and economic variables that shape ideal and real role expectations
- The personal characteristics of the superintendents themselves

Often these influences interact to the extent that isolating their separate effects at any given point becomes virtually impossible.

With regard to general environments and organizational dynamics, the second chapter of this book reviewed the evolution of urban school districts. Historians and scholars in educational administration have provided a clear picture displaying that big-city school systems have generally been resistant to organizational restructuring despite massive transitions in their ecosystems. (See Resource D for a discussion of governance structures and attempts at reform.) The lack of adaptations in both culture and climate has led many scholars to retain their characterizations of urban schools as bureaucratic organizations in that power remains centralized, administration continues to be structured in multiple layers of authority, and real community needs rarely serve as catalysts for programmatic change.

Districts we now call "urban" are not, however, a homogeneous group. Some are extremely large in enrollment and geographic territory, whereas others have fewer than 30,000 students and encompass relatively few square miles. Some are experiencing rapid declines in enrollment; others are actually among the fastest growing school districts in America. Some are less bureaucratic than others. But beyond such differences, these complex organizations share several major problems. All have high populations of students living in poverty, all have growing minority populations, and all face serious financial problems.

This final chapter addresses the future of the urban superintendency and challenges that lie ahead. Included are comments from Arthur Steller, deputy superintendent of the Boston Public Schools and currently president of the Association for Supervision and Curriculum Development. His input was obtained in interviews conducted in the spring and summer of 1994. Steller has served as superintendent in all types of school districts, including a major urban district (the Oklahoma City Public Schools), and his insights provided another dimension to this study.

The Present

Unlike big-city superintendents 50 years ago, virtually all of whom were white males from relatively small towns (in 1958, only 2% came from very large cities), today's urban school chiefs are a heterogeneous group. Many are female (approximately 15%-18%) and minorities (approximately 60%-65%). Some are best described as "upwardly mobile" individuals with a strong career orientation. They tend to spend considerable time outside of their districts, and they are realistic about the improbability of staying in their current positions for a prolonged period. Others are individuals who have never worked in a district other than the one they now head. These individuals tend to spend much of their time within the district, and they usually express tremendous loyalty to their current positions.

Although slightly over half of the superintendents I studied indicated that they had never set the goal of becoming an urban superintendent, this pattern was certainly not consistent among all 17. When asked to comment on this finding, Arthur Steller noted that he had established the objective of becoming an urban superintendent as early as age 16. He further noted that he set his sights on reaching the position by age 35.

In a book on the school superintendency written over two decades ago, Carlson (1972) broadly categorized school superintendents as being either place bound or career bound. The former group included individuals who were rather passive toward the specific goal of becoming a superintendent and were not highly inclined toward job mobility (i.e., changing employers to achieve promotions). By contrast, those in the former category engaged in deliberate career planning, accepted mobility as part of their career development, and were likely to be appointed to the superintendency as "outsiders" when conditions within the school district were deemed to be unsatisfactory. Generally, the superintendents in the Reference Group were slightly more apt to fit Carlson's definition of *place bound*—a finding that certainly was not anticipated.

When asked why they entered and remained in the job, most of the superintendents from whom I collected data indicated a dedication to playing a key role in helping children in urban areas. Steller, who knows the vast majority of individuals who have served in this capacity over the last 10 years, affirmed that this is essentially true. It is difficult, however, to separate dedication from personal interests—and persons who acquire the urban superintendency have ample opportunities to gain fame and a relatively good salary. Although I did not collect data on the "afterlife" of urban superintendents, there is considerable evidence that many of them eventually move to equally or more lucrative positions with private corporations, foundations, or government service. Two quite recent examples involve superintendent turnover in Detroit and San Diego. In the former, Superintendent Deborah McGriff resigned to accept an executive position with the Edison Project, a company developing profit-making schools ("Detroit Official," 1993), and in the latter, Superintendent Thomas Payzant resigned to accept a high-ranking position with the U.S. Department of Education. Although not all former big-city superintendents move to highly lucrative or desirable positions, few, if any, return to teaching at radically reduced salaries—a condition that is rather common for superintendents who end their administrative careers in small, rural districts. Further research may reveal that opportunities created by having served in the urban superintendency may, in fact, attenuate career-related concerns about the limited probability of surviving in the job for more than 3 years.

Regardless of difficulties that may exist between school boards and superintendents, it is apparent that many urban superintendents continue to have a certain level of power. Studies of work behavior provide some verification that superintendents are constrained by community and organizational conditions, but this condition does not prevent many of them from exerting influence over organizational decisions and outcomes (Pitner & Ogawa, 1981). I asked Steller about my finding that most of the superintendents in the Reference Group relied heavily on their own views in making critical decisions (a factor found to be second only to financial considerations in making decisions). Again, he found no reason to disagree, but he offered a caveat about pushing a personal agenda without regard for either timing or politics.

> If you are to survive very long, you have to temper your convictions with appropriate timing and be willing to wait— to make some decisions at a later time than you may like. You have to play your cards carefully—keep some things moving forward—but other things, because the timing is not right— you may have to put them on hold for a period of time. That's an issue I don't think a lot of people have particularly mastered—and I'm not saying that I totally mastered it either. Circumstances are sometimes overwhelming. That certainly is a key ingredient in how you temper your convictions. There

is a critical element of the job that entails framing—or marketing—your convictions to other audiences.

There is a fine line between the professional responsibility to provide direction and the bureaucratic inclination to make decisions unilaterally, and Steller's observation points out the importance of being able to understand that line of demarcation. Frequently, big-city superintendents are placed in no-win situations in which both decisiveness and democratic procedures generate criticism. Taking charge and accepting responsibility for difficult decisions, the administrator may be labeled a dictator. Inviting widespread participation and sharing power, he or she is judged to be "wishy-washy," or criticized for not providing professional direction.

Politics is a central theme in virtually all discussions of the urban superintendency. Most members of the Reference Group affirmed that they had experienced tough, "hardball" politics, and several specific examples were cited earlier in the book. Steller again agreed that politics were pervasive in big-city school administration. He gave the following explanation:

> Some of the urban politics may be the climate itself. In a city you have more special-interest groups, you have more diversity, and you have more community neighborhood activists. And they are different from activists you may encounter in suburban areas. I mean, I've been in both situations—as well as rural areas—and it's just a different climate in urban settings. The odds are that in an urban area you have more individuals who come from that activist, special interest segment of the public who actually get appointed or elected to the board than in suburban districts—although some of that is changing in nonurban areas. The suburban boards are not the same as they used to be either—and they are becoming more political.

Are urban districts as bad as most people believe? Over 80% of the superintendents in the Reference Group thought that big-city school systems were unfairly judged by the public. Steller generally agreed with them, but noted, "The problems are certainly serious.

They are not quite as bad as the media portray them, but that does not mean that they can be ignored. Urban educational problems can be tackled and resolved. I'm convinced they can."

Approximately two out of three superintendents in the Reference Group expressed the opinion that the general public really wants urban schools to improve. Yet reform efforts to date have been largely nonintegrative and nonsystemic; they have been predicated on the notions that (a) schools are largely responsible for the problems they face, and (b) schools can improve without corresponding changes in the community and social environments. In light of problems such as poverty, crime, and violence, this seems to be a very misguided conclusion. When asked directly about reform issues, urban super-intendents expressed a degree of enthusiasm—but when asked to generally identify problems and challenges, reform was hardly mentioned. This may reflect their cynicism that reform to date has largely centered on political responses that are easy to understand, but that ignore the systemic implications of big-city problems.

A recent report based on a 1993 survey of leadership in the Council of Great City Schools, *Critical Educational Trends: A Poll of America's Urban Schools* (Ottinger & Root, 1994), showed that societal problems are usually seen by superintendents as more pressing than school reform. Violence, gang-related activity, a lack of parent involvement, bilingual education, and non-English-speaking students were all listed ahead of school reform and site-based management as the most pressing issues facing urban schools.

Before conducting the interviews for this book, I thought that the superintendents would be preoccupied with ideas that related to forcing public schools to be more competitive. More to the point, I expected them to talk extensively about vouchers, charter schools, tuition tax credits, and other ideas that are designed to provide alternatives to the public schools. Instead, what I heard centered largely on issues that can be classified as "those essentially beyond the control of the superintendents and even their school boards." They are issues such as poverty, federal and state funding of public education, crime, and the like.

In reviewing the nature of the communities, the school districts, and the superintendents, I found that generalizations were far more feasible at the organizational level than at either the environmental or the personal level. More precisely, the structure and organizational patterns of urban school districts showed greater commonalities than did either the communities or the superintendents. This observation is critically important, because the culture and climate of organizational life have extensive effects on the prescribed and actual roles assumed by superintendents. For this reason, the immutability of urban school districts is one of the central issues that should dominate discussions about the future.

The Future

There are ample reasons to doubt whether some urban school districts will survive. The term *downsizing* was a recurring theme voiced by many of the superintendents in both their surveys and their interviews. Discussing the difficulty of dealing with diminishing resources, one superintendent put it this way:

> I mean, everybody is talking about downsizing now—at a time when, you know, you need people to deliver services. And you're downsizing here and downsizing there, and cutting this and cutting that at a time when those millions of dollars in lost resources should be enhancing programs for students who come to us.

When asked about resources, another superintendent said,

> We've been in a downsizing mode for the last 7 or 8 years, and that downsizing has primarily occurred at the central office level. . . . We have attempted to streamline, become more efficient—to downsize—at a time when the demands and expectations are increasing.

Over the past three decades, some urban districts have lost thousands of students, not only because of outmigration, but also as a result of court-ordered, one-way busing programs. The assessed valuations in some large cities have actually declined, and since the early

1980s, there has been a growing sentiment that radical measures are needed to improve urban districts.

Frustrations have resulted in several recommendations that threaten the very existence of urban school districts. The most prominent have been concepts that focus on competition, initiatives such as choice and vouchers, and charter schools. Critics charge that forcing inadequately funded urban schools to compete with wealthier suburban districts will only serve to intensify racial and economic segregation (e.g., Fowler-Finn, 1993-1994). Advocates of competition, by comparison, share a common perception that improvement is probably impossible under the current governance structures of urban districts. Nathan Glazer (1993), for example, declared that big-city bureaucracies have become an ineffective structure given the drain of social problems that affect children from poor and troubled homes. Proposing school choice as a more efficacious alternative, he wrote:

It is a model that frightens many school people and supporters of public schools, but if schools of the central cities, the schools that deal with the black and Hispanic children who make up a large and growing part of our school population, are to improve, it is hard to see any other alternative that can be effective. (p. 648)

Those who advocate competition are indirectly promoting the transition of public schooling to the private sector of the economy—a change that replaces decisions made on behalf of society with decisions made largely on the basis of self-interest. Paul Hill (1994), for example, suggested that reform efforts such as choice, vouchers, and charter schools can be only partially effective because they are not a complete alternative to the existing governance structure. Thus he concluded that they are more likely to be transformed by the system than to transform it. He advocated private contracting—an idea advanced by Myron Lieberman (1986) in his thought-provoking book *Beyond Public Education*. More recently, the idea has been popularized by efforts such as the Edison Project and Education Alternatives, Incorporated—a for-profit company that has stressed better management as a means of improving schools. Although the idea of competition is appealing, the economic implications of placing all or parts of the education enterprise in the private sector of the economy need to be studied in greater detail.

Schlechty (1990) took yet another position on concepts such as vouchers and choice, suggesting that they do not offer meaningful solutions to the education problems in urban schools. He predicted that such efforts will neither change the behavior of school boards nor lead to the total demise of big-city districts:

> Instead, over the long term, American education might well end up with a two-level system—one for the affluent and concerned, run by private corporations and churches, and one for groups often labeled "at risk" and those who have no effective choice because of transportation problems or lack of information. School boards will run the latter system. (p. 27)

Even proposals of choice that attempt to neutralize family wealth and reward effort (e.g., family power equalization—a concept developed by Coons and Sugarman, 1978) have been rejected by many educators who believe that much of the middle class and most of the more wealthy will find ways to use vouchers or tuition tax credits to create a tiered system of schools.

Finally, there are those who suggest that urban districts should be gerrymandered out of existence. That is, the city systems should be eradicated and their territory divided among several surrounding suburban districts. Or city systems should be absorbed into all-county districts that essentially merge suburban and city districts into an even larger organization.

But what do urban superintendents see as the future for their school organizations? What is their vision for their own jobs in the 21st century? I posed these questions to the members of the Reference Group. Although the responses uniformly suggested that more difficult times were ahead, the reasons given represented multiple perspectives.

> I don't think urban districts will become extinct. I think they will have different governing structures, and we are likely to see academy schools, charter schools, and the like. You will still have the urban district, but you'll have separate entities

operating portions of the program—and these entities will still be under the auspices and control of the district school board.

I think the urban superintendency will become increasingly complex. I do not see the tenure of superintendents lengthening, primarily because of the many societal factors that urban districts must deal with. However, I think there will be those in the education profession who will attempt to get these jobs—but I'm not sure they will do so for the right reasons. Because in some instances people are only interested in the status, power, and dollars that go with the job. I don't have a lot of optimism about the urban superintendency becoming any less complex or any easier. I think it will become more difficult unless there is some kind of a change in the support from the general community, community leaders, and boards of education. It's such a difficult job that I think few people are going to be able to tolerate the complexities of the job for very long.

I think the future is going to be very rocky at best. And then you've got the whole issue of how are you going to finance schools. That ties back to the larger issue of what I call "the shrinking political constituency for public schools." When you look at who attends school versus who pays and who votes, the lessons that we learn from our referendum [defeat of a school financing measure] keep hitting us in the face. The problems children bring to school are still growing, and this keeps making things even more difficult. In my opinion, it's not a bright future. Somehow we need to create changes and to get people into key positions and allow them to stay long enough so that they can actually make a difference. I now understand clearly why people only stay in these jobs for 2 years, or two and one-half years, or whatever the average is. . . . And the rapid turnover makes things worse. Because you have this constant change in top leadership, and the superintendents don't really control the districts. All of this instability impacts negatively on the districts.

One problem with urban districts is the superintendents themselves. Not the boards, not any other single variable. I think
it is the superintendents. I'm probably the only person to
stand up and say this, and I've said it to them. Because I really
don't see urban superintendents being advocates for children. I see urban superintendents playing the political role
to maintain their jobs—and trying to be well liked in a country club atmosphere or at the Rotary or Lions. I don't see
urban superintendents rolling up their sleeves and getting in
there to battle for children. And I think this is a weakness of
the profession. So when you deal with those other issues,
that's when you become vulnerable to the political pitfalls.
Ten years ago, the pioneers were people like Art Jefferson in
Detroit and Alonzo Crim in Atlanta. Today, not enough pace-
setters in the Council of Great City Schools are really advocating for children. I'm very critical of superintendents—very
critical. I get calls from superintendents every day, well, maybe
not every day, but two or three times a week. And they ask
me why I'm saying things like this. And I respond, "Why
don't you say it too, dammit?" They tell me they are afraid.

Whether urban districts survive depends on the basic economics and social conditions in America. I think that right
now the cities in America are literally tinderboxes—especially when you look at data that pertain to large cities. And
this really has nothing to do with superintendents—or how
large or how small schools are. It has nothing to do with
accelerated learning or whether we are using the Coalition
of Essential Schools model. We see increasing numbers of
children for whom every day is literally a fight for survival,
and parents who don't know what the children are doing,
who are in an almost hopeless state when it comes to controlling or taking care of their children. The alienation that
exists toward society in general is something that schools
will have difficulty overcoming—regardless of organizational
models or instructional models. And this is a frightening situation. We just had a couple of very shocking stories unfold
in our city—and we're not one of the real big cities like Chi-

cago or Los Angeles. But the police picked up an 8-year-old kid who was selling "crack." This kid was himself addicted to cocaine. Eight years old! Selling drugs in one of our city parks. And during the same week, a 14-year-old girl was standing in front of her home talking to friends at 10 or 11 p.m. Someone drove by and shot her—one of those drive-by shootings—and the young girl was killed. The editor of the newspaper asked the chief of police, the head of a welfare agency, and me if we saw any connections between the two incidents. The chief said it was poverty and all the conditions that poverty breeds. The woman from the welfare agency focused on the shame of violence in big cities. I said it was a sense of hopelessness among parents and among so many young people—hopelessness that leads to alienation and vindictive action against other individuals. The editor took these concepts and weaved them into an interesting and searching article that would pertain to any large city in America. If there is one lesson that history has taught us, it is that schools are not typically change agents. Schools reflect values and society. Consequently it is extremely difficult for schools to really be successful with children who live in this milieu. And unless we have some dramatic changes in our cities, I see extreme difficulties for urban education in the future.

Steller believes that urban districts probably will survive, but only if they are able to adjust to become more responsive and flexible. Commenting specifically about the governance structure of these organizations, he noted:

Urban boards have not necessarily outlived their usefulness— although in their current form and with their tendency to micro-manage, they do not deserve to survive. The present governance structure of school districts should not be viewed as something that ought to survive for its own sake. There ought to be a reason why any approach to school stewardship, including the existing one, survives. The rationale should be . . . because it is providing better governance than other alternatives, . . . not simply because it is a particular model or tradition.

He went on to say that there are growing signs that school boards, per se, may not weather the storm in some cities.

In the midst of criticism, there are mounting signs that some urban school boards have reached the point of taking unprecedented risks. In late 1993, for example, the Minneapolis School Board voted to turn over the management of its school system to Public Strategies Group, Incorporated—a private management group (Jordan, 1993b).

In addition, a growing number of big-city school boards are looking over their shoulders to observe the growing impatience of state officials. As was proven in Chicago in the late 1980s, when urban school problems become state problems, legislatures and/or governors will intervene, and their frustrations often engender drastic measures. More recently, an example of state interference was exhibited when New Jersey's education commissioner moved to take fiscal control of the Newark school system by appointing a special auditor to oversee the district's financial operations. This individual was given veto power over any school board action that involved spending more than $20,000 (Strum, 1993). Pipho (1988) noted that when city officials engage in the political issues of urban schooling, the outcomes are unpredictable, "but when city and state officials move in concert to change a large-city school district, events become more unpredictable" (p. 398). And because the actions of state officials may well ignore the systemic realities of public schooling—for both political and economic reasons—their final stage of intervention may include legislative actions that dissolve urban districts as we now know them.

The Challenges

This book has provided a closer look at 17 urban school superintendents and their work environments. In concluding, several major challenges deserve review. They are a mix of community-, organization-, and profession-based concerns. Writing about the brief tenures of urban superintendents, *Washington Post* columnist Mary Jordan

(1993a) stated that the brief tenure of urban school chiefs underscored how the job had become a flashpoint for mounting urban social problems, soaring public demands, and increased political backbiting. Many who have studied the conditions of urban schooling readily agree with her assessment, and consequently they judge that the position of big-city school chief cannot be understood properly unless it is examined in the context of practice (i.e., the communities and school districts in which these individuals work).

Learning More About Superintendents

Given the stature and importance of the school superintendency, it is indeed disappointing that so little attention has been given to studying this position. A richer understanding is dependent on well-designed studies that probe how variables within school districts and the broader environment of the community interact with personal variables to shape work behavior. Are superintendents most influenced by personal values and beliefs? To what extent do precepts, concepts, and experiences gained in professional education influence behavior?

Because organizational transformation is a paramount issue in urban schooling, we especially need to establish more informed views regarding successful practice in this area. For example, how does longevity affect inclinations of superintendents to pursue change in their school districts? What successful practices appear to have applicability to all or most urban school districts?

In addition, we really should know more about "life after the urban superintendency." From a career perspective, what happens to these individuals when they are dismissed or resign? How many move on to even more lucrative positions? At present there is considerable speculation that competent individuals are lured to big-city superintendencies by the assured visibility—which ultimately becomes a springboard to a more desirable post with a foundation, private business, or the like. Data reported here, however, suggest a strong commitment to the profession in general and the superintendency in particular. Not all move to jobs in universities or foundations.

One reason why there has been so little research on the superintendency is that it is difficult to execute. This is especially true of qualitative research that probes the subtleties of practice in relation to specific conditions. In the next few years, there ought to be more concerted efforts to examine the interactivity of person, organization, task, and community.

Recreating the Image of Superintendents

From the earliest days of urban school districts, administrators and professors of educational administration have sought to separate management from teaching. Although there have always been forward-thinking scholars who have challenged this initiative, the value of dividing the profession has been seriously questioned in the past 10 to 15 years. One of the most thought-provoking pieces on this topic was authored by Sergiovanni (1991). Suggesting that reform may bring both teacher professionalism and decentralized governance, he cautioned that administrators may not be well served by further distancing themselves from teachers. If teachers truly become empowered, principals and superintendents may be more effective if they are viewed as professional leaders rather than professional managers.

Cuban's study (1976) of three urban superintendents who served in the 1950s and 1960s brought to light how professional beliefs, socialization, and conflicting organizational demands served to shape their behavior. All of the men he studied had previous experience as teachers for 12 or more years. This part of their lives probably had a profound influence on their ability to assume the role of educational leader.

Today, far too many citizens only see the managerial side of administration. When I asked the superintendents in the Reference Group if their school boards really expected them to be instructional leaders, 29% said always, 53% said occasionally, and 18% said rarely or never. It is truly questionable whether either politics or management can play a lesser role in the lives of urban school chiefs as long as the tiered bureaucracy with its centralization of power remains intact.

Logically, urban superintendents must wear three hats. They must be skilled politicians; they must be effective managers; but first and foremost, they ought to be scholars who are respected for their professional knowledge, analytical skills, and planning capabilities. The current trend toward contracting school districts or individual schools to management firms raises fundamental questions about the very essence of professional education. Factors that force or encourage practitioners to spend all of their time resolving conflict and managing resources need to identified and altered. For when the value of the superintendency is described as political and managerial, deductive reasoning leads many taxpayers to believe that those specifically trained in politics and management may be able to do the job more effectively.

Finally, we need to come to precise understandings about the meaning of professionalism. At least two very different views are emerging in the context of school reform. One casts professional superintendents as individuals of vision and superior knowledge who enter organizations with the specific intention of implementing their ideas and goals. The other characterizes them as leaders who bring colleagues together to address problems democratically and to collectively set an agenda for the future—a view that often describes administrators as "firsts among equals." These two perceptions of professionalization entail more than differences in leadership style, and until there is greater consensus on the more desired role, the urban superintendency is likely to remain mired in politics.

Dealing With Known Governance Problems

The past 15 years of attempted reform have opened many eyes to the reality that public schools are not likely to improve if they remain structurally intact. Discussing research on school boards, Danzberger (1994) indicated that these bodies frequently become dysfunctional "because of conflicts between members and the resulting incapacity to chart a clear direction for their school systems" (p. 370). She added that many board members often lack common perceptions of what a school board ought to do and their specific responsibilities as members.

Because communities, including big cities, are unique entities, it is unlikely that any universal prescription for reshaping the governance of school districts will suffice. In some central cities, moving from elected to appointed boards may produce improvement. Other cities may require more radical measures. Regardless of the proposals that may be produced, it is critical to protect the "public" nature of our schools. There simply are too many potential dangers associated with placing such a vital institution in the private sector of the economy.

As the problems of urban districts become more severe, there are mounting temptations to sacrifice liberty for adequacy and equity. In all probability, change can be accomplished more readily if it is imposed either by state mandates or by the views of a select few "experts." But what price must we pay? Are we willing to abandon local control completely? I think not, so I agree with Steller's conclusion that school boards have not outlived their usefulness. What is needed, however, is a reconceptualization of their role—changes that will allow decisions to be influenced more by professional knowledge and less by big-city politics.

Balancing Centralization and Decentralization

Today, decentralization is being advanced and accepted as a solution even though we know relatively little about the ultimate educational benefits that may be produced. Manifest conflicts are often swept aside as if they had little relevance or the power to deter real change. Teacher professionalism and democratic decision processes (as advanced in site-based management) offer a splendid example. To what extent are parental and student input to be limited in order to grant greater professional control over what occurs in schools?

There is a reality in practice that superintendents quickly learn. It focuses on accountability and responsibility. Those who head school districts are expected to maintain reasonable control over both resources and programs. Fullan's work (1991) on educational change reminds us that neither centralization nor decentralization is the answer to school improvement.

Murphy (1991) aptly observed that the long-standing image of superintendents as power figures with all the wisdom and answers was rendered inefficacious by the cumulative circumstances resulting from the dispersal of power and knowledge, the competing interests of multiple constituencies, a growing mistrust of government, and the concurrent application of decentralization and professionalization. As schools are given greater independence, as teachers acquire power to control their practice, and as parents and other taxpayers are integrated into the decision-making process, a different image of the successful superintendent is likely to emerge.

Concentrating on the Causes and Not the Symptoms

Some problems plaguing our central cities will not be resolved regardless of the level of improvement in public schools. Poverty, the dilemma of children rearing children, and gang violence are symptomatic of deep-rooted social problems that are steadily worsening in America. For literally millions of young people, the entertainment industry, professional sports, and other parts of "pop culture" have supplanted the family as the sources of values and beliefs. And neither repeated condemnations nor massive federal programs have been able to reverse this unwelcome trend.

Social ills are not, however, an excuse for urban schools to remain as they are. Although some big-city schools are effective, and although there are thousands of dedicated teachers and administrators working in those schools, the fact remains that many are dismal and dangerous places. The worst of them are little more than holding places for children and adolescents who are neither challenged nor encouraged to grow intellectually.

Two realities should dominate the next decade of reform. First, improvements are most likely if they are systemic—they should address both social and educational problems simultaneously. They should involve partnership ventures between cities and schools. Second, improvement is more likely if it planned and executed at the micro level. Federal and statewide reforms often have only minimal relevance for urban schools. Even district-wide efforts may prove to be ineffectual in large cities with diverse neighborhoods. This challenge, like the others, will not be easily met, because the needs of our youth must compete for scarce resources in cities that already are woefully lacking in resources.

Sustaining Effective Leadership

Put simply, we must remove the revolving door from the urban superintendent's office. No organization can be expected to engage in meaningful reforms when there is a change in top leadership every 2 or 3 years. Far too often, strong and capable leaders are forced from office in order to satisfy pressure groups or to reassure the public that change is imminent. Perhaps urban school superintendents ought to receive contracts in relation to long-term plans and initiatives. More specifically, they ought to be employed on the basis of their philosophy and ability to bring people to a common vision; they ought to be held accountable for the results; and they should be given reasonable time parameters to complete their objectives.

It is ironic that coaches in professional sports often are accorded more opportunity to succeed than are big-city superintendents. Some survive four or five dismal seasons before their rebuilding efforts come to fruition. In an organization where the stakes are much higher, we must educate the public to the reality that schools will not improve by periodically changing superintendents. The idea that one individual can successfully transform a complex organization by imposing his or her vision in a relatively short period of time is simply myopic (Fullan, 1991).

Finding New Purposes for Education

Perhaps none of the challenges outlined here can be addressed adequately unless communities are able to reach consensus on new purposes for public education. Futurists warn that life in the next century will be harsh on those who lack the skills and knowledge necessary in an Information Age. Yet approximately one third of all students fail in our public schools (Schlechty, 1990). That is, either they do not graduate or they receive a diploma even though they are functionally illiterate (and these statistics are much more alarming when urban schools are considered in isolation).

The problems created by a growing number of undereducated citizens, most of whom are living in poverty, are already becoming clear. American society, in general, faces a difficult test. The nation is at risk, but not just because of public education. In part, contemporary urban schools are not achieving their potential because they are being pulled in too many different directions; they are expected to do far too much with far too few resources. Unless communities can successfully embrace new and realistic purposes for their public schools, these institutions may not survive.

Membership in the Council
of Great City Schools—1993

Anchorage (AK) Public Schools*
Baltimore City Public Schools
Broward County (FL) Public Schools
Chicago Public Schools
Cleveland Public Schools
Dade County (FL) Public Schools
Dayton (OH) Public Schools
Detroit Public Schools
East Baton Rouge Parish Schools*
Fresno (CA) United Schools
Indianapolis Public Schools
Los Angeles Unified School District
Memphis City Schools
Minneapolis Public Schools
New Orleans Public Schools
Norfolk Public Schools
Oklahoma City Public Schools
Philadelphia Public Schools
Portland Public Schools
Sacramento Unified School District
St. Paul (MN) Public Schools
San Francisco Unified School District
Toledo Public Schools
Washington (DC) Public Schools

Atlanta Public Schools
Boston Public Schools
Buffalo Public Schools
Cincinnati Public Schools*
Columbus (OH) Public Schools
Dallas Independent School District
Denver Public Schools
Duval County (FL) Public Schools*
El Paso (TX) Independent School District
Houston Independent School District
Jefferson County (KY) Public Schools
Long Beach (CA) United School District
Milwaukee Public Schools
Nashville Davidson Metro Public Schools
New York City Public Schools
Oakland (CA) Unified School District
Omaha Public Schools
Pittsburgh Public Schools
Rochester (NY) City Schools
St. Louis Public Schools
San Diego Unified School District
Seattle Public Schools
Tucson Unified Schools

*Districts not included in the March 1993 membership list provided by the Council of Great City Schools but appearing in previous reports about the council.

153

Participating Superintendents

School District	State	Superintendent
Atlanta Public Schools	GA	Lester Butts
Broward County Public Schools	FL	Virgil L. Morgan
Buffalo Public Schools	NY	Albert Thompson
Cleveland Public Schools	OH	Sammie Campbell Parrish
Columbus Public Schools	OH	Lawrence Mixon
Dade County Public Schools	FL	Octavio J. Visiedo
Dayton Public Schools	OH	James Williams
Denver Public Schools	CO	Evie Dennis
Fresno Unified Schools	CA	Charles E. McCully
Houston Public Schools	TX	Frank Petruzielo
Indianapolis Public Schools	IN	Shirl E. Gilbert II
Jefferson County Public Schools	KY	Donald Ingwerson
Milwaukee Public Schools	WI	Howard Fuller
New York City Public Schools	NY	Joseph Fernandez
Omaha Public Schools	NB	Norbert Schuerman
St. Louis Public Schools	MO	David Mahan
Washington Public Schools	DC	Franklin Smith

Participating Districts

T he influence of large school systems in America is illuminated by the fact that the 100 largest constitute less than 1% of all school districts but educate 23% of all students and employ 23% of all teachers in public elementary and secondary education (Sietsema, 1993). These massive school systems are often referenced with the adjectives *urban* or *big-city*. In certain respects, these labels are accurate and useful, because they permit us to group school systems that are usually very large (in terms of student enrollment) and functioning within the boundaries of our largest cities. Unfortunately, they also serve to strengthen the generalization that all organizations in the group are essentially alike.

In reality, districts classified as urban show considerable variation. For instance in several southern states, elementary and secondary public education is organized into single county school districts— that is, there is only one school district per county. Florida, Kentucky, and Louisiana are examples. Many of the school districts in these states are large, in both land mass and enrollment—and some, but not all, include major cities (e.g., Miami in Dade County, Florida, or Louisville in Jefferson County, Kentucky).

In collecting data from the Reference Group, several questions were raised about the school districts, communities, and school boards. This was done to determine the extent of community and organizational variation that existed.

TABLE RC-1 Participating School Districts

State	District	Enrollment	Number of Schools
California	Fresno	77,000	93
Colorado	Denver	63,100	106
Georgia	Atlanta	59,550	109
Florida	Broward County	179,795	190
	Miami	302,163	279
Indiana	Indianapolis	46,553	85
Kentucky	Louisville	93,411	153
Missouri	St. Louis	40,842	102
Nebraska	Omaha	43,150	75
New York	Buffalo	48,200	77
	New York City	989,000	1,100
Ohio	Cleveland	72,000	127
	Columbus	63,688	141
	Dayton	27,700	50
Texas	Houston	198,750	244
Wisconsin	Milwaukee	100,158	158
Other	District of Columbia	80,937	178

Size of Districts

The 17 superintendents included in my study were employed in districts spread across the United States. Twelve states and the District of Columbia were represented. These districts are identified in Table RC-1, which also provides information about district enrollment and the number of schools included in each district.

As these data exhibit, there was considerable variation both in terms of total student enrollment and in terms of the number of schools operated. New York City, for example, is massive when compared to Dayton, St. Louis, or Omaha. Yet all districts were large when compared to school districts in general.

Enrollment Patterns

In the period of 1989 to 1993, the districts in the Reference Group also had varying enrollment patterns. Given the frequently voiced concern about declining populations in major cities, it was somewhat surprising that none reported an enrollment decline over 10% during this 5-year span. A report issued by the Council of Great City Schools for school year 1990-91 showed that the school-age population (5- to 17-year-olds) in the 47 member school districts declined about 8.5% from 1980 to 1990. This decline occurred even though several larger districts, most notably in the Southeast, were growing at a rather rapid pace. The 47 districts making up the Council of Great City Schools enrolled 13.1% of all public school students in 1990-91—a percentage that remained constant from the 1980-81 school year (Casserly, 1992).

Enrollments during the 1991-92 school year in member districts of the Council of Great City Schools ranged from a low of approximately 28,000 to a high of just over 950,000 pupils. A majority of districts had enrollments below 100,000 pupils (National Center for Education Statistics, 1993).

In the 17 districts included in my study, approximately 59% reported enrollment increases: 17.6% reported increases in excess of 10%, 29% reported enrollment declines of less than 10%, and the remainder (12%) reported stable enrollments. Broward County (Fort Lauderdale, Florida) reported an enrollment increase in the past 3 years of approximately 21,000 students. School officials there noted that this trend was likely to continue, especially if the federal government persisted with its present immigration policies.

Even though a number of big-city districts have had declining enrollments over the past two decades, 85% of the superintendents in the Council of Great City Schools in 1994 indicated that they expected overall increases in school enrollments in the next 5 years. They anticipated these increases at both the elementary and secondary school levels (Ottinger & Root, 1994). Given the current economic and social trends in many large cities, reasons for their optimism were not readily apparent.

Ethnic/Racial Composition

Today, about 22% of the total population in America can be described as minority; however, 30% of the school-age children are in this category—and shortly after the year 2000, that figure is expected to reach 36% (Hodgkinson, 1993). Approximately half of the largest 100 school districts in the United States had over 50% minority enrollments during the 1990-91 school year (Sietsema, 1993).

Aggregate 1990-91 school year data for the 47 school districts in the Council of Great City Schools revealed the following distribution: 42.1% African American, 25% white, 26.5% Hispanic, 5.9% Asian American, and 0.5% Alaskan/Native American. Even more revealing were the facts that nearly 4 out of every 10 African American students and 1 out of every 3 Hispanic students attending public schools in that year were enrolled in one of these 47 districts (Casserly, 1992).

Table RC-2 provides total enrollment data and minority enrollment data reported by the U.S. Department of Education for the school year 1991-92. Only member districts of the Council of Great City Schools are included here. Data were not reported for Phoenix, and minority data were not reported for either Atlanta or Norfolk.

Data in Table RC-2 show that all of the districts reporting have over 25% minority enrollment. Even more revealing is the fact that 80% of the 44 districts reporting minority enrollments reported "minority-majorities."

Demographic data provided by 16 of the 17 school systems in the Reference Group provided more insight into the composition of minority student populations. For example, 90% of the students in Washington, D.C., were identified as African American (that means that approximately another 8% are classified as other minorities), but only 29% of the students in Omaha and 22% of the students in Denver were identified as African American (even though Denver has an overall minority student population of 67%). Hispanic populations also varied substantially among the 17 districts. In Houston and Dade County, 48% of the students were identified as Hispanic, but seven other districts reported Hispanic populations of less than 5%. Variation was also found with regard to Caucasian populations. Omaha reported that 68% of the student enrollments was Caucasian, whereas Washington, D.C., and Atlanta reported 4% and 7%, respectively. New York City, the largest district in the United States, reported a Caucasian student population of only 19%.

A growing number of experts are bringing to light the fact that race is not necessarily the most critical demographic factor facing

TABLE RC-2   Percent of Minority Pupils During the 1991-92
School Year

District	Total Enrollment	% of Minority Pupils
Anchorage	44,749	26.9
Atlanta	59,905	—
Baltimore	110,325	82.7
Boston	60,922	79.1
Broward County	170,032	44.4
Buffalo	48,241	60.0
Chicago	409,731	88.4
Cincinnati	50,914	64.4
Cleveland	71,640	77.2
Columbus	63,723	51.6
Dade County	304,545	81.6
Dallas	137,746	84.1
Dayton	27,798	64.0
Denver	60,552	67.0
Detroit	169,320	92.3
Duval County	115,940	41.0
E. Baton Rouge	62,946	57.7
El Paso	64,728	78.7
Fresno	74,693	68.7
Houston	196,689	86.3
Indianapolis	47,136	53.4
Long Beach	74,048	74.1
Los Angeles	636,964	86.9
Memphis	105,005	80.0
Milwaukee	93,381	69.8
Minneapolis	41,597	53.7
Nashville	69,103	41.1
New Orleans	83,847	93.1
New York	962,269	81.5
Norfolk	37,323	—
Oakland	51,698	91.8
Oklahoma City	36,097	56.0
Omaha	42,536	34.8
Philadelphia	195,735	77.3
Phoenix	—	—
Pittsburgh	40,384	58.3
Portland	54,496	29.0
Rochester	33,792	73.8

(continued)

TABLE RC-2 Continued

District	Total Enrollment	% of Minority Pupils
Sacramento	50,804	65.7
St. Louis	40,956	79.6
St. Paul	34,265	44.7
San Diego	123,591	64.5
San Francisco	61,689	86.1
Seattle	44,423	56.8
Toledo	39,720	45.1
Tucson	56,764	48.0
Washington, D.C.	80,618	96.0

SOURCE: National Center for Education Statistics, 1993.

urban schools. Bracey (1993), for one, identified social and economic factors as more important. Discussing a research study that found that only one in four public school students in the 47 largest school districts was white, he wrote, "These statistics, of course, mask the real problem, because they present the situation in terms of race. But race and ethnicity are proxy variables for the real problem: class" (p. 111). In the realm of social and economic class distinctions, the mounting concerns that middle and upper class African Americans, Hispanics, and other minorities are abandoning urban schools is certainly noteworthy. The proclivity of more affluent minority families to move to the suburbs is the economic equivalent of "white flight."

Pupils Per Teacher, Student Performance, and Expenditures for Education

Data from the 1990-91 school year exhibited that vast differences existed in the average per-pupil expenditures among districts in the Council of Great City Schools. In addition, data analyzed from the following school year revealed substantial differences among these districts with regard to average class sizes (or more precisely, student-teacher ratios). Information on student-teacher ratios is shown in Table RC-3, and figures regarding per-pupil expenditures are found in Table RC-4.

TABLE RC-3 Number of Classroom Teachers and Pupils Per Teacher: 1991-92 School Year

District	Classroom Teachers	Pupils Per Teacher
Anchorage	2,117	21.1
Atlanta	3,943	15.2
Baltimore	5,900	18.7
Boston	—	—
Broward County	9,129	18.6
Buffalo	3,119	15.5
Chicago	22,676	18.1
Cincinnati	3,035	16.8
Cleveland	3,666	19.5
Columbus	3,972	16.0
Dade County	15,651	19.5
Dallas	8,292	16.6
Dayton	1,709	16.3
Denver	3,707	16.3
Detroit	—	—
Duval County	5,756	20.1
E. Baton Rouge	3,919	16.1
El Paso	3,740	17.3
Fresno	3,261	22.9
Houston	11,006	17.9
Indianapolis	2,622	18.0
Long Beach	2,982	24.8
Los Angeles	27,635	23.0
Memphis	5,334	19.7
Milwaukee	5,554	16.8
Minneapolis	2,255	18.4
Nashville	3,943	17.5
New Orleans	4,671	18.0
New York	53,279	18.1
Norfolk	2,399	15.6
Oakland	2,264	22.8
Oklahoma City	2,158	16.7
Omaha	2,561	16.6
Philadelphia	10,798	18.1
Phoenix	—	—
Pittsburgh	2,472	16.3
Portland	2,800	19.5
Rochester	2,313	14.6

(continued)

TABLE RC-3 Continued

District	Classroom Teachers	Pupils Per Teacher
Sacramento	2,179	23.3
St. Louis	3,114	13.2
St. Paul	1,778	19.3
San Diego	5,279	23.4
San Francisco	3,068	20.1
Seattle	2,235	19.9
Toledo	2,235	17.8
Tucson	2,698	21.0
Washington, D.C.	4,672	17.3

SOURCE: National Center for Education Statistics, 1993.

Pupil-teacher ratios are commonly used to compare school systems because they are a convenient and rather straightforward statistic. Increasingly, however, critics of public education are refusing to accept either class sizes or per-pupil expenditures as legitimate indices of educational effectiveness. Rather, they are demanding hard proof; they want to see specific student outputs. Bracey (1993) cited several examples of statistics generated by recent research studies that do not bode well for urban schools:

- Comparing the performance of seventh-grade "A" students on standardized tests, researchers found that those in high-poverty schools (i.e., schools with 75% or more students receiving free lunches) scored only in the 36th percentile in reading and 35th percentile in mathematics; by contrast, seventh-grade "A" students in low-poverty schools (i.e., those with 6% to 20% free lunches) scored in the 81st and 86th percentiles, respectively.
- In Washington, D.C., public schools, only 60% of the students graduate from high school and about 25% of them take the Scholastic Aptitude Test (SAT). Yet average scores for these students in 1993 were only 336 on the verbal portion and 369 on the mathematics portion (compared to 1993 national averages of 424 on the verbal portion and 478 on the mathematics portion). These scores indicate that the students, on average, provided correct answers

TABLE RC-4 Expenditures Per Pupil: 1990-91 School Year

District	Expenditures Per Pupil	Rank in Group[a]
Anchorage	$5,803	17
Atlanta	5,971	14
Baltimore	4,665	34
Boston	7,791	3
Broward County	5,440	22
Buffalo	7,324	6
Chicago	4,898	31
Cincinnati	6,044	12
Cleveland	6,593	8
Columbus	5,891	15
Dade County	5,788	18
Dallas	4,083	41
Dayton	6,471	9
Denver	4,998	29
Detroit	4,722	33
Duval County	4,509	37
E. Baton Rouge	4,126	39
El Paso	3,429	45
Fresno	4,594	36
Houston	3,667	43
Indianapolis	4,999	28
Long Beach	4,641	35
Los Angeles	5,832	16
Memphis	3,400	46
Milwaukee	6,603	7
Minneapolis	5,974	13
Nashville	3,813	42
New Orleans	4,104	40
New York	7,380	5
Norfolk	5,114	27
Oakland	5,232	25
Oklahoma City	3,519	44
Omaha	4,900	30
Philadelphia	5,756	19
Phoenix	—	—
Pittsburgh	7,931	2
Portland	6,137	11
Rochester	8,866	1
Sacramento	4,725	32

(continued)

TABLE RC-4 Continued

District	Expenditures Per Pupil	Rank in Group[a]
San Diego	5,363	23
San Francisco	5,170	26
Seattle	5,660	20
St. Louis	6,394	10
St. Paul	5,470	21
Toledo	5,291	24
Tucson	4,239	38
Washington, D.C.	7,383	4

SOURCE: National Center for Education Statistics, 1993.
a. Excluding Phoenix, for which no data were provided.

for approximately 33% of verbal items and 25% of the mathematics items. Because the test is multiple choice, a person guessing on each item would be expected to get 20% correct just by guessing. As outputs come under close scrutiny, there are rising suspicions that both grade inflation and low standards exist in many urban schools. A study in the late 1980s indicated that "even the 'best' students from an inner city high school produced SAT scores of about 700 in total" (Stout, 1993, p. 297).

With regard to the pupils-to-teacher ratios, it is noteworthy that the large school districts in the western part of the United States had the highest figures. Of those reporting ratios of 20:1 or higher, all were in the West except Duval County, Florida, which had a ratio of 20.1:1. Perhaps even more noteworthy is the fact that all six California districts were above the 20:1 figure.

Wide differences also existed with regard to per-pupil expenditures, and although this might partially be explained by cost-of-living effects, it is doubtful that this is the major reason for the variance. For instance, San Diego and San Francisco are among cities with the highest costs of living, yet their per-pupil expenditures are basically average when compared to others in the group (the average for all 46 reporting was $5,450). The five districts that reported per-pupil expenditures below $4,000 were all in the South or Southwest (El Paso, Houston, Nashville, and Oklahoma City).

Finally, it is noteworthy that Rochester, New York, had the highest average per-pupil expenditure, $8,866, and the lowest pupils-to-teacher ratio, 14.6:1, among the school districts included in Tables RC-3 and RC-4. During the 1980s, this district received substantial media exposure related to its planned organizational transitions that included school-based planning and shared decision making. Many were quick to praise the efforts of both school officials and union leaders in Rochester. In part, the adulation was influenced by the fact that change efforts in this district were moving against the contemporary currents of reform. Rather than accept the notion that intensification mandates could sufficiently improve schooling, officials in Rochester sought to restructure the control mechanisms in their district. The newly developed working relationship among the teachers' union, the superintendent, and the school board—a coalition forged out of trust, but laden with risk—was an especially frequent target of praise. A contract settled with the teachers' union in the late summer of 1987 called for substantially higher teacher salaries and detailed major aspects of the reform program that included the Career in Teaching Program and school-based planning (Koppich, 1992).

Teachers salaries in Rochester are now among the highest in the nation, and although many still cite the district as a reform model because of decentralized governance, skeptics are beginning to question what the community has received for its investment. At some point in the not-too-distant future, it is inevitable that both researchers and policy makers will examine more closely the cost-benefit ratios in public school districts that had significant spending increases in the past decade. The evidence they produce not only will shed light on the perennial arguments focusing on the relationships between spending and educational outcomes, but also is likely to influence future reform initiatives in urban schools.

Socioeconomic Composition

Data generated by the U.S. Bureau of the Census reveal the strong relationship between race and income in America. In 1991, for instance, approximately 21% of all children in this country were reported to be living in families below the poverty level (this compares with only 14.9% in 1970). Yet 45.6% of African American children and 39.8% of Hispanic children fell into this category (National Center for Education Statistics, 1993).

During 1993, the trend toward higher numbers of children living in poverty continued. Nearly one in every four children in America was living below the poverty line—a condition that puts them at grave risk of not fulfilling their physical and mental promise (Hodgkinson, 1993). There is a widely held perception that urban schools serve many of these children, and there is ample evidence to support this conclusion. Demographic data from the 17 school districts in the Reference Group showed that across all them, slightly more than half of the students were identified as living in low socioeconomic circumstances.

Although some districts had substantially more students in the low-income category than others, every district reported that at least one in four children came from low-income families (the lowest reported was 27%). In six of the districts, at least two out of three students were reported to come from low-income families. At the other end of the spectrum, only one district, Broward County, reported that over 20% of the students enrolled came from upper middle or upper class families (15% from upper middle and 10% from upper).

As noted previously, many observers now believe that socioeconomic class is a more critical issue for urban schools than race because of the increasing tendency for affluent minority families to move from inner-city environments. This demographic pattern has created a downward economic spiral that threatens the very survival of some big cities. School officials in these environments have had to face two realities: that their districts are no longer serving a predominately middle-class population, and that they must find ways to withstand shrinking tax bases (McCurdy & Hymes, 1992). The needs of students living in poverty almost always require added resources. School officials understand that these students will be best served by full-service schools that provide social, psychological, and physical support, but they are far less certain how this can be accomplished when the standard measure of school district wealth (assessed valuation) is being eroded. The worst scenario occurs in those districts that are simultaneously experiencing (a) the flight of middle-class families, (b) a decline in taxable property, and (c) an increase in student population, usually due to immigrant families who live in poverty conditions.

Governance Structures

Organizational Structure

For the most part, the administrative structure of urban school districts is essentially as it was four decades ago. True, districts such as Chicago, Boston, New York, and Dade County have attempted decentralization programs, but these efforts have yet to produce a model that has been widely embraced by other urban districts. Although each of these efforts to change long-standing governance structures in big-city school districts is unique, and although there have been varying degrees of success, reform efforts in the largest school systems have generally served to exhibit the tremendous immutability of large bureaucracies.

The decentralization plan for the city schools in Chicago is a good case in point. Neither the idea nor the directive to establish school and district councils came from the school board or administration; it was imposed by the Illinois state legislature (in legislation known as the Chicago Reform Act). This imposed restructuring was expected to reduce centralized authority, redistribute power, and provide schools with direct access to resources. Studying implementation of the plan, English (1990) described the effort as "an example of the concept of organizational rationality, the notion that shifting the goals and objectives for a system will ultimately change its behavior and actions, and the results or outcomes will be different or improve" (pp. 6-7). His personal work as a consultant to the Chicago School Finance Authority, a statutory body responsible for overseeing fiscal operations and the implementation of the reform effort, led him to conclude that the approach in Chicago made it nearly impossible to reform anything. His final judgment was, "Grass roots or not, Chicago's 'business as usual' is quite likely to remain the same business" (p. 21).

Disappointments also have been expressed with regard to efforts to dismantle the bureaucracy in New York City. Over the decades there have been numerous attempts to reform this school system, and although some have produced positive outcomes, they have generally left the administrative structure intact. Cronin (1973) provided one such example when he detailed how school officials some years back sought independence from political party bosses. In achieving their goal, the administrators had neither restructured their organization nor made it free from politics; they had merely established the school system as a separate, independent political force.

Upon his arrival as chancellor of the New York City Schools, Joseph Fernandez declared an all-out assault on the bureaucratic structure. He eliminated tenure for building principals, brought down the Board of Examiners (a 92-year-old process that Fernandez said only got in the way of progress and affirmative action), and moved some schools toward site-based management (Fernandez & Underwood, 1993). But these minor victories did not topple the long-standing problems of centralized power. Anne Lewis (1994), a noted education writer, declared that a change in structure did not ensure a change in administrative practices: "As the experience in New York City demonstrates, decentralization is not a panacea for the ills of poor leadership" (p. 357).

Writing about the bureaucratic nature of urban schools in the early 1970s, Levine (1973) concluded that the same forces and problems that caused failures in other rational bureaucracies, such as hospitals, industrial companies, and municipal service departments, were deterring the effective delivery of public elementary and secondary education in urban areas. More specifically, he cited the following as the most critical problems:

- Institutional complexity and overload (internal structures are either too complex or rendered inoperable when large burdens are placed on them)
- Goal displacement (the goal of self-perpetuation outweighs other purposes)

- Deficiencies in communication and decision-making processes (a condition created by multiple layers of administration/ management)
- Social and psychological distance between client and organization (those who operate the schools lose touch with the real needs of the community) (pp. 245-246)

Today, urban districts are described in varying ways, but most scholars who study the organizational nature of schools and school districts agree that urban districts maintain structural elements of bureaucracy (e.g., centralized authority). They also agree, however, that loose coupling and the quasi-professional status of educators are conditions contrary to bureaucratic operations.

Profile of the School Boards

In recent years, efforts to restructure public schools have indirectly increased attention on urban school boards. More to the point, there has been an increasing level of questioning with regard to whether the traditional role of school boards should be sustained (e.g., Harrington-Lueker, 1993; Todras, 1993). Discussing problems with school boards, Danzberger (1994) noted that toward the end of the last decade hopes for improved student achievement began to wane as meaningful change was not evident. She cited urban schools as presenting an especially bleak picture in this regard, and noted that citizens had questioned virtually every aspect of public schooling except the local institution that governed them. Among the common criticisms of school boards she identified were a failure to take political risks that may be necessary for reform to occur, a tendency to engage in micromanagement, a failure to exercise adequate policy oversight, a reliance on rhetoric rather than action, a lack of attention to performance, and an incapacity to develop positive and productive relationships with the superintendent.

There is mounting evidence that the behavior of urban school board members is atypical. A recent study by Newman and Brown (1993), for instance, showed that size of school district often influences the degree to which board members are dependent on the recommendations of the superintendent. Those in large-enrollment districts indicated that they "used superintendents' recommendations less to resolve conflicts than did board members from medium or small districts" (p. 277). That is, urban school board members are often more independent and directly involved in problems.

Such observations are frequently supported by comments from superintendents themselves. A 1992 article in *Sounding Board*, a newsletter that reports on urban school districts, included the following passage: "The consensus among superintendents is that there is a new breed of board members whose characteristics have changed dramatically in the last few years. Some board members have insisted on becoming more and more involved in administration rather than in policy formulation" ("Superintendent-School Board Relations," p. 4). The article quotes several anonymous sources as saying that urban board members are now often younger and more apt to see their role as more analogous to that of legislators. They want to become immersed in problems by taking testimony from taxpayers and school employees.

Former New York City chancellor Joseph Fernandez provided a vivid description of the political activities of a big-city school board in his book *Tales Out of School* (Fernandez & Underwood, 1993). He concurred with findings from a March 1992 study released by the National Schools Boards Association that found that many school board members were micro-managing. Many individuals who had successfully placed themselves on these governing bodies were seen as having personal agendas that led them to intrude into administrative activities to advance their own political interests. According to Fernandez, such behavior was a major factor in the rapid turnover rate of superintendents nationally.

Rather than being perceived as a stabilizing and supporting force that permits meaningful change to occur, urban boards are often portrayed as dysfunctional and an obstacle to reform. Increasingly, those who leave the position of urban school chief exhibit a proclivity to make harsh public statements about their former school board members. They charge that these individuals are preoccupied with either personal political ambitions or the dissatisfactions and objectives of the pressure groups they represent.

An early 1990s study conducted by the Institute for Educational Leadership pointed out that many board members believe they are weakest in areas that are critical to meaningful organizational change, such as instructional policy or links with other community leaders (Danzberger, Kirst, & Usdan, 1992). Schlechty (1992) suggested that one of the greatest obstacles to school reform is the fact that too many school board members view themselves as political figures and too few accept the roles of moral and cultural leaders. It is precisely for such reasons that many reformers are beginning to question whether urban school boards are, in themselves, a barrier to change. Danzberger and Usdan (1994), for example, found little disagreement among experts with regard to the argument "that it is time to focus attention on the local governing system and on school boards in particular" (p. 366). Such calls for scrutiny have sparked several notable questions. Are urban school boards structured differently from other school boards? Is the need for change greater in urban districts than in other types of school systems?

Evidence shows that urban boards are not structurally unique. Data reported by the Council of Great City Schools in 1992 indicated that:

- 6 of 47 member school districts (12.8%) had appointed school boards
- The number of board members in the districts varied from 5 to 13
- The mode for the number of school board members was 7 (55% had seven-member school boards) (Casserly, 1992)

A 1990 study of school districts with enrollments over 33,500 found that the seven-member school board was the mode. In addition, it was established that:

- Males constituted 58% of board members
- Minorities constituted about 28% of the board members
- Nearly 90% of the districts elected school board members (Ornstein, 1992)

School board elections are not, however, conducted uniformly across large school systems. Among the member districts in the Council

TABLE RD-1 Profile of School Board Size and Selection in the
Reference Group

District	Number of Members	Method of Selection
Atlanta, GA	9	Nonpartisan election
Broward County, FL	7	Partisan election
Buffalo, NY	9	Nonpartisan election
Cleveland, OH	7	Nonpartisan election
Columbus, OH	7	Nonpartisan election
Dade County, FL	7	Partisan election
Dayton, OH	7	Nonpartisan election
Denver, CO	7	Nonpartisan election
Fresno, CA	7	Nonpartisan election
Houston, TX	9	Nonpartisan election
Indianapolis, IN	7	Nonpartisan election
Louisville, KY	7	Nonpartisan election
Milwaukee, WI	9	Nonpartisan election
New York City, NY	7	Appointed
Omaha, NB	12	Nonpartisan election
St. Louis, MO	12	Nonpartisan election
Washington, D.C.[a]	11	Nonpartisan election

a. Does not include a nonvoting student representative who is a 12th member.

of Great City Schools, 16 elect members solely on an at-large basis, 16 have elections in which members are chosen solely by district or ward, and 7 have elections in which member selection is achieved through a combination of at-large and district/ward arrangements (Casserly, 1992).

Figures for size of school boards and method of selection held pretty much true for the 17 school districts in Reference Group. These data are provided in Table RD-1. Chicago, which was not part of the Reference Group, had the largest school board in the Council of Great City Schools with 15 members, and five of the member districts in this organization (Long Beach, New Orleans, San Diego, Toledo, Tucson) had five-member school boards (Casserly, 1992).

Although the structure and roles of school boards are a pervasive concern in public education, the need to create more appropriate policy mechanisms is more urgent in big cities than it is elsewhere.

Danzberger (1994) concluded that the long-standing organization of school boards has become ineffective in the context of emerging issues and challenges. She wrote, "Reforms must occur because this 18th century institution, reformed only once in the early 20th century, is not structurally suited to govern effectively in an increasingly divisive society that is facing unprecedented economic and social challenges" (p. 371). The only real organizational change in urban school districts in nearly 150 years has been a change from massive school boards to boards of more manageable size—and this change occurred during the Industrial Revolution era.

REFERENCES

Ascher, C. (1991). *Retaining good teachers in urban schools.* (ERIC Document Reproduction Service No. ED 341 762)

Bennett, D. A. (1991). Big-city blues. *American School Board Journal, 178*(4), 22-24.

Berman, B. (1983). Business efficiency, American schooling, and the public school superintendency: A reconsideration of the Callahan thesis. *History of Education Quarterly, 23,* 297-321.

Blumberg, A. (1985). *The school superintendent: Living with conflict.* New York: Teachers College Press.

Boaz, D. (1991). The public school monopoly: American's Berlin Wall. In D. Boaz (Ed.), *Liberating schools: Education in the inner city* (pp. 1-50). Washington, DC: CATO Institute.

Boothe, J. W., Bradley, L. H., & Flick, T. M. (1994). This working life. *Executive Educator, 16*(2), 39-42.

Boyan, N. J. (1988). Describing and explaining administrator behavior. In N. Boyan (Ed.), *Handbook of research in educational administration* (pp. 77-98). New York: Longman.

Bracey, G. W. (1993). The third Bracey Report on the condition of public education. *Phi Delta Kappan, 75,* 104-117.

Burbank, N. B. (1969). *The superintendent of schools: His headaches and rewards.* Danville, IL: Interstate.

Burlingame, M. (1988). The politics of education and educational policy: The local level. In N. Boyan (Ed.), *Handbook of research in educational administration* (pp. 439-451). New York: Longman.

175

Burroughs, W. A. (1974). *Cities and schools in the gilded age*. Port Washington, NY: Kennikat.

Button, H. W. (1991). Vulnerability: A concept reconsidered. *Educational Administration Quarterly, 27*(3), 378-391.

Butts, R. F., & Cremin, L. A. (1953). *A history of education in American culture*. New York: Henry Holt.

Callahan, R. E. (1962). *Education and the cult of efficiency*. Chicago: University of Chicago Press.

Campbell, R. E., Cunningham, L. L., Nystrand, R. O., & Usdan, M. D. (1990) *The organization and control of American schools* (6th ed.). Columbus, OH: Charles E. Merrill.

Carlson, D. (1993). The politics of educational policy: Urban school reform in unsettling times. *Educational Policy, 7*(2), 149-165.

Carlson, R. O. (1972). *School superintendents: Careers and performance*. Columbus, OH: Charles E. Merrill.

Carnegie Foundation for the Advancement of Teaching. (1988). *An imperiled generation: Saving urban schools*. Lawrenceville, NJ: Princeton University Press.

Casserly, M. (1992). *National urban education goals: Baseline indicators, 1990-91*. (ERIC Document Reproduction Service No. ED 351 422)

Cawelti, G. (1982). Guess what? Big city superintendents say their school boards are splendid. *American School Board Journal, 169*(3), 33-35.

Celis, W. (1993, February 17). Heads of big-city schools need political skills to last. *New York Times*, p. B9.

Coons, J. E., & Sugarman, S. D. (1978). *Education by choice: The case for family control*. Berkeley, CA: University of California Press.

Corwin, R. G., & Borman, K. M. (1988). School as workplace: Structural constraints on administration. In N. Boyan (Ed.), *Handbook of research on educational administration* (pp. 209-237). New York: Longman.

Council of Great City Schools. (1986). *The condition of education in the Great City Schools: A statistical profile, 1980-1986*. Washington, DC: Author.

Council of Great City Schools. (1992). *Superintendent characteristics*. Washington, DC: Author.

Cremin, L. (1961). *The transformation of the school: Progressivism in America, 1876-1957*. New York: Knopf.

Crisci, P. E., & Tutela, A. D. (1990). Preparation of educational administrators for urban settings. *Urban Education, 24,* 414-431.

Cronin, J. M. (1973). *The control of urban schools.* New York: Free Press.

Crowson, R. L. (1987). The local school district superintendency: A puzzling role. *Educational Administration Quarterly, 23*(3), 49-69.

Cuban, L. (1976). *Urban school chiefs under fire.* Chicago: University of Chicago Press.

Cuban, L. (1985). Conflict and leadership in the superintendency. *Phi Delta Kappan, 67,* 28-30.

Cubberley, E. P. (1922). *Public school administration.* Boston: Houghton-Mifflin.

Cunningham, L. L., & Hentges, J. T. (1982). *The American school superintendency 1982: A summary report.* Arlington, VA: American Association of School Administrators.

Dahl, R. A. (1969). Leaders in public education. In M. Gittell & A. Hevesi (Eds.), *The politics of urban education* (pp. 145-154). New York: Praeger.

Danzberger, J. P. (1994). Governing the nation's schools: The case for restructuring local school boards. *Phi Delta Kappan, 75,* 367-373.

Danzberger, J. P., Kirst, M. W., & Usdan, M. D. (1992). *Governing public schools: New times, new requirements.* Washington, DC: Institute for Educational Leadership.

Danzberger, J. P., & Usdan, M. D. (1994). Local educational governance. *Phi Delta Kappan, 75,* 366.

Daresh, J. C., & Playko, M. A. (1992, April). *Aspiring administrators' perceptions of the superintendency as a viable career choice.* Paper presented at the annual meeting of the American Educational Research Association, San Francisco.

Deal, T., Lison, C., & Deck, L. (1993). Exits and entrances. *School Administrator, 50*(5), 26-28.

Detroit official joins for-profit schools venture. (1993, October 15). *New York Times,* p. 19.

Dewey, J. (1899). *The school and society.* Chicago: University of Chicago Press.

Duignan, P. (1980). Administrative behavior of school superintendents: A descriptive study. *Journal of Educational Administration, 18*(1), 5-26.

Eaton, W. E. (1990). The vulnerability of school superintendents: The thesis reconsidered. In W. Eaton (Ed.), *Shaping the superintendency: A reexamination of Callahan and the cult of efficiency* (pp. 11-35). New York: Teachers College Press.

English, F. W. (1990, October). *Can rational organizational models really reform anything? A case study of reform in Chicago.* Paper presented at the meeting of the University Council for Educational Administration, Pittsburgh, PA.

ERS Staff Report. (1985). Characteristics of public school superintendents. *ERS Spectrum, 4*(4), 28-31.

Farquhar, R. H. (1977). Prepatory programs in educational administration. In L. Cunningham, W. Hack, & R. Nystrand (Eds.), *Educational administration: The developing decades* (pp. 329-357). Berkeley, CA: McCutchan.

Fernandez, J. A., & Underwood, J. (1993). *Tales out of school: Joseph Fernandez's crusade to rescue American education.* Boston: Little, Brown.

Fiedler, F. E., & Chemers, M. M. (1974). *Leadership and effective management.* Glenview, IL: Scott, Foresman.

Fowler-Finn, T. (1993-1994). Why have they chosen another school system? *Educational Leadership, 51*(4), 60-62.

Friesen, D., & Duignan, P. (1980). How superintendents spend their working time. *Canadian Administrator, 19*(5), 1-5.

Fullan, M. (1991). *The new meaning of educational change* (2nd ed.). New York: Teachers College Press.

Getzels, J. W., & Guba, E. G. (1957). Social behavior and the administrative process. *School Review, 65*, 423-441.

Glass, T. E. (1992). *The 1992 study of the American school superintendency: America's education leaders in a time of reform.* Arlington, VA: American Association of School Administrators.

Glazer, N. (1992). The real world of urban education. *Public Interest,* (106), pp. 57-75.

Glazer, N. (1993). American public education: The relevance of choice. *Phi Delta Kappan, 74*, 647-650.

Goldstein, A. (1992). Stress in the superintendency: School leaders confront the daunting pressures of the job. *School Administrator, 49*(9), 8-11.

Gouldner, A. W. (1958). Cosmopolitans and locals: Toward an analysis of latent social roles. *Administrative Science Quarterly, 2,* 281-306.

Greene, K. R. (1990). School board members' responsiveness to constituents. *Urban Education, 24,* 363-375.

Griffiths, D. E. (1966). *The school superintendent.* New York: Center for Applied Research in Education.

Haberman, M. (1989). More minority teachers. *Phi Delta Kappan, 70,* 777-779.

Hallinger, P., & Murphy, J. (1993). Developing leaders for tomorrow's schools. *Phi Delta Kappan, 72,* 514-520.

Hanson, E. M. (1991). *Educational administration and organizational behavior* (3rd ed.). Boston: Allyn & Bacon.

Harrington-Lueker, D. (1993). Reconsidering school boards. *American School Board Journal, 180*(2), 30-36.

Hill, P. T. (1994). Reinventing urban public education. *Phi Delta Kappan, 75,* 396-401.

Hodgkinson, H. (1991). Reform versus reality. *Phi Delta Kappan, 73,* 8-16.

Hodgkinson, H. (1993). American education: The good, the bad, and the task. *Phi Delta Kappan, 74,* 619-625.

Holmes, M. (1991). The values and beliefs of Ontario's chief education officers. In K. Leithwood & D. Musella (Eds.), *Understanding school system administration* (pp. 154-174). Philadelphia: Falmer.

Hosman, C. M. (1990). Superintendent selection and dismissal: A changing community defines its values. *Urban Education, 25,* 350-369.

Hummel, R. C., & Nagle, J. M. (1973). *Urban education in America: Problems and prospects.* New York: Oxford University Press.

Hunter, R. C. (1990). The big city superintendent: Up against an urban wall. *School Administrator, 47*(5), 8-11.

Involving cities in our schools (1993). *Sounding Board, 2*(1), 1-2, 5.

Jackson, B. L., & Cibulka, J. G. (1992). Leadership turnover and business mobilization: The changing political ecology of urban school systems. In J. G. Cibulka, R. J. Reed, & K. W. Wong (Eds.), *The politics of urban education in the United States* (pp. 71-86). Philadelphia: Falmer.

Jacobson, S. L. (1989). School management: Still a white man's game. *Executive Educator, 11*(11), 19.

Jones, E. H., & Montenegro, X. P. (1990). *Women and minorities in school administration*. (ERIC Document Reproduction Service No. ED 273 017)

Jordan, M. (1993a, February 13). Big city school chiefs learn reform is not 1 of the 3 Rs. *Washington Post*, pp. A1, A7.

Jordan, M. (1993b, November 5). Minneapolis votes to hire firm to run city schools. *Washington Post*, p. 1.

Judge, T. A., & Watanabe, S. (1993). Another look at the job satisfaction-life satisfaction relationship. *Journal of Applied Psychology, 78,* 939-948.

Katz, M. (1993). Matching school board and superintendent styles. *School Administrator, 50*(2), 16-17, 19-20, 22-23.

Kirst, M. W., & McLaughlin, M. (1990). *Rethinking children's policy: Implications for educational administration*. Bloomington: Indiana University, Consortium on Educational Policy Studies.

Knezevich, S. J. (1962). *Administration of public education*. New York: Harper & Brothers.

Koppich, J. E. (1992). *The rocky road to reform in Rochester*. (ERIC Document Reproduction Service No. ED 346 557)

Kowalski, T. J., & Reitzug, U. C. (1993). *Contemporary school administration: An introduction*. New York: Longman.

Kozol, J. (1967). *Death at an early age: The destruction of the hearts and minds of Negro children in the Boston public schools*. Boston: Houghton Mifflin.

Kozol, J. (1991). *Savage inequalities: Children in America's schools*. New York: Crown.

Kozol, J. (1992). Flaming folly. *Executive Educator, 16*(4), 14-19.

Krinsky, I. W., & Rudiger, C. W. (1991). The lure of the big time. *Executive Educator, 13*(9), 29-31.

Lasher, G. C. (1990). Judgment analysis of school superintendent decision making. *Journal of Experimental Education, 59*(1), 87-96.

Leithwood, K. A., Steinbach, R., & Raun, T. (1993). Superintendents' group problem-solving processes. *Educational Administration Quarterly, 29,* 364-391.

Levine, D. U. (1973). Concepts of bureaucracy in urban school reform. In T. Glass (Ed.), *Crisis in urban schools* (pp. 244-252). New York: MSS Information Corporation.

Lewis, A. C. (1994). Reinventing local school governance. *Phi Delta Kappan, 75,* 356-357.

Lieberman, M. (1986). *Beyond public education.* New York: Praeger.

Lipham, J. M. (1988). Getzels's models in educational administration. In N. Boyan (Ed.), *Handbook of research on educational administration* (pp. 171-184). New York: Longman.

Maeroff, G. I. (1988). Withered hopes, stillborn dreams: The dismal panorama of urban schools. *Phi Delta Kappan, 69,* 633-638.

Makedon, A. (1992). Reform and traditional public school: Toward a typology of conservative to radical reforms. *Illinois Schools Journal, 72*(1), 15-22.

Manch, J. (1976). The urban superintendency as viewed by a survivor. *Phi Delta Kappan, 58,* 348-349.

March, J. G., & Simon, H. A. (1958). *Organizations.* New York: John Wiley.

McCloud, B., & McKenzie, F. D. (1994). School boards and superintendents in urban districts. *Phi Delta Kappan, 75,* 384-385.

McCord, R. S., & Kops, G. C. (1992). Executives' pay linked to market. *School Administrator, 11*(49), 36.

McCurdy, J., & Hymes, D. L. (1992). *Building better board-administrator relations.* Arlington, VA: American Association of School Administrators.

McKelvey, T. V. (1969). Urban school administration: Some problems and futures. In T. McKelvey & A. Swanson (Eds.), *Urban school administration* (pp. 197-214). Beverly Hills, CA: Sage.

Milstein, M. M. (1992). The overstated case of administrator stress. *School Administrator, 49*(9), 12-15.

Morris, J. R. (1979). Job(s) of the superintendency. *Educational Research Quarterly, 4*(4), 11-24.

Murphy, J. T. (1991). Superintendents as saviors: From the Terminator to Pogo. *Phi Delta Kappan, 72,* 507-513.

Murphy, J. (1992). *The landscape of leadership preparation: Reframing the education of school administrators.* Newbury Park, CA: Corwin.

National Center for Educational Statistics. (1993). *Digest of education statistics 1993.* Washington, DC: U.S. Department of Education, Office of Educational Research and Improvement.

National Policy Board for Educational Administration. (1989). *Improving the preparation of school administrators: An agenda for reform.* Charlottesville, VA: Author.

Newman, D. L., & Brown, R. D. (1993). School board member role expectations in making decisions about educational programs:

Do size of school and region of country make a difference? *Urban Education, 28,* 267-280.

Ornstein, A. C. (1991). Problems facing school superintendents and school board presidents of large school districts. *Urban Review, 23,* 207-214.

Ornstein, A. C. (1992). School superintendents and school board members: Who are they? *Contemporary Education, 63*(2), 157-159.

Ortiz, F. I. (1991, April). *Superintendent leadership in urban schools.* Paper presented at the American Educational Research Association, Chicago.

Ortiz, F. I., & Marshall, C. (1988). Women in educational administration. In N. Boyan (Ed.), *Handbook of research in educational administration* (pp. 123-142). New York: Longman.

Ottinger, C., & Root, M. (1994). *Critical education trends: A poll of America's urban schools.* Washington, DC: Council of Great City Schools.

Oxley, D. (1994). Organizing for responsiveness: The heterogeneous school community. In M. Wang & E. Gordon (Eds.), *Educational resilience in inner-city America: Challenges and prospects* (pp. 179-190). Hillsdale, NJ: Lawrence Erlbaum.

Paddock, S. C. (1981). Male and female career paths in school administration. In P. Schmuck, W. Charters, & R. Carlson (Eds.), *Educational policy and management of sex differentials* (pp. 187-198). New York: Academic Press.

Payne, C. M. (1984). *Getting what we ask for: The ambiguity and failure in urban education.* Westport, CT: Greenwood.

Penner, D. (1993, December 4). Gilbert says he didn't ask for Florida job. *Indianapolis Star,* pp. B1-2.

Penner, D., & Hooper, K. L. (1994, May 22). IPS board fires Gilbert, who had yet to resign. *Indianapolis Star,* pp. 1-2.

Pink, W. T. (1992). The politics of reforming urban schools. *Education and Urban Society, 25*(1), 96-113.

Pipho, C. (1988). Urban school districts and state politics. *Phi Delta Kappan, 69,* 398-399.

Pitner, N. J., & Ogawa, R. T. (1981). Organizational leadership: The case of the school superintendent. *Educational Administration Quarterly, 17*(2), 45-65.

Portner, J. (1994, January 12). School violence up over past 5 years, 82% in survey say. *Education Week, 13*(16), 9.

Rada, R. D. (1984). Community dissatisfaction and school governance. *Planning and Changing, 15*(4), 234-247.

Reaves, J. A. (1994). Trebelhorn shows courage after loss. *Chicago Tribune*, April 30, p. D1.

Renchler, R. (1992). Urban superintendent turnover: The need for
stability. *Sounding Board, 1*(1), 1-3.

Rist, M. C. (1984). Superintendents: Here's how you work, live, play,
and think. *Executive Educator, 6*(9), 26-30.

Rist, M. C. (1990). Race and politics rip into the urban superintendency. *Executive Educator, 12*(12), 12-15.

Rochester, M. J. (1993, December 8). Gilbert takes self off Florida school
post list. *Indianapolis Star*, pp. 1-2.

Schaefer, R. J. (1990). Footnotes on Callahan's Teachers College. In W.
Eaton (Ed.), *Shaping the superintendency: A reexamination of Callahan
and the cult of efficiency* (pp. 36-66). New York: Teachers College Press.

Schlechty, P. C. (1990). *Schools for the twenty-first century: Leadership
imperatives for educational reform.* San Francisco: Jossey-Bass.

Schlechty, P. C. (1992). Deciding the fate of local control. *American
School Board Journal, 178*(11), 27-29.

Scott, H. J. (1976). The urban superintendency on the brink. *Phi Delta
Kappan, 58*, 347-348.

Scott, H. J. (1980). *The black school superintendent: Messiah or scapegoat?*
Washington, DC: Howard University Press.

Scott, H. J. (1990). Views of black school superintendents on black
consciousness and professionalism. *Journal of Negro Education,
59*(2), 165-172.

Sergiovanni, T. J. (1991). The dark side of professionalism in educational administration. *Phi Delta Kappan, 72*, 521-526.

Sietsema, J. (1993). *Characteristics of the 100 largest public elementary
and secondary school districts in the United States: 1990-91.* (ERIC
Document Reproduction Service No. ED 359 226)

Spring, J. (1985). *American education: An introduction to social and political aspects* (3rd ed.). New York: Longman.

Spring, J. (1990). *The American school: 1642-1990* (2nd ed.). New York:
Longman.

Stout, R. T. (1993). Establishing the mission, vision, and goals. In P.
Forsyth & M. Tallerico (Eds.), *City schools: Leading the way* (pp. 287-
318). Newbury Park, CA: Corwin.

Strum, C. (1993, May 14). Trenton names auditor to rule Newark schools. *New York Times*, p. 1.

Superintendent-school board relations. (1992). *Sounding Board 1*(1), 4-5.

Tallerico, M. (1989). The dynamics of superintendent-school board relationships: A continuing challenge. *Urban Education, 24,* 215-232.

Tallerico, M. (1993). Governing urban schools. In P. Forsyth & M. Tallerico (Eds.), *City schools: Leading the way* (pp. 211-252). Newbury Park, CA: Corwin.

Tallerico, M., Poole, W., & Burstyn, J. N. (1994). Exits from urban superintendencies: The intersection of politics, race, and gender. *Urban Education, 28,* 439-454.

Tanner, C. K. (1989). Positive educational policy with negative impacts on students. *High School Journal, 72*(2), 65-72.

Thomas, W. B., & Moran, K. J. (1992). Reconsidering the power of the superintendent in the Progressive Period. *American Educational Research Journal, 29*(1), 22-50.

Todras, E. (1993). *The changing role of school boards.* (ERIC Document Reproduction Service No. ED 357 434)

Trotter, A., & Downey, G. W. (1989). Many superintendents privately contend school board "meddling" is more like it. *American School Board Journal, 176*(6), 21-25.

Tyack, D. (1972). The "One Best System": A historical analysis. In H. Walberg & A. Kopan (Eds.), *Rethinking urban education* (pp. 231-246). San Francisco: Jossey-Bass.

Tyack, D., & Hansot, E. (1982). *Managers of virtue: Public school leadership in America, 1820-1980.* New York: Basic Books.

Viteritti, J. P. (1986). The urban school district: Toward an open system approach to leadership and governance. *Urban Education, 21,* 228-253.

Wesson, L. H., & Grady, M. L. (1994). An analysis of women urban superintendents: A national study. *Urban Education, 28,* 412-424.

Wiggins, T. (1988). Stress and administrative role in educational organizations. *Journal of Educational Research, 82*(2), 120-125.

Willower, D. J. (1979-1980). School superintendents and their work. *Administrator's Notebook, 28*(5), 1-4.

Wilson, J. C. (1991). Making it in the big city. *Executive Educator, 13*(9), 31-33.

Winerip, M. (1994, April 10). Recent turmoil in New York City schools is history repeating itself, only faster. *New York Times*, p. 1.

Zlotkin, J. (1993). Rethinking the school board's role. *Educational Leadership, 51*(2), 22-25.

INDEX